LUST
FOR
GOLD

"O Cursed Lust for Gold, to what dost thou not drive the hearts of men!"

Virgil.

LUST FOR GOLD

GARRY HOGG

19953

New York: A. S. Barnes and Co.

First American Edition 1962

For
JEAN MAULDON
In Gratitude
For Many Hours
of
Tedious Research

9808
Printed in the United States of America

CONTENTS

ACKNOWLEDGEMENT

The quotations on pages 141, 143 and 145 from *The Tomb of Tutankhamen* by Howard Carter are printed by courtesy of the publishers, Cassell & Co., Ltd. The copyright of the illustrations is held as follows: nos. 2, 3, 4, 5 and 14, *Radio Times* Hulton Picture Library; nos. 6, 7, 8 and 15, Keystone Press; nos. 1, 11 and 12, the Mansell Collection; nos. 9 and 10, Associated Press; no. 13, The Victoria and Albert Museum.

LIST OF ILLUSTRATIONS

Introduction

It is an odd paradox that gold, which has been more highly prized and more greatly coveted by man than any other metal throughout the thousands of years since he first discovered it, should also be one of the most widely distributed of metals.

It is, of course, to be found in very many rocks in most parts of the world. Usually it exists only in minute quantities: as gold dust, in quartz "lodes", as grains, as microscopic particles, scales, or "plates", and in "dirt" carried down from auriferous rocks denuded by streams or weather; it is, however, occasionally found in the form of nuggets substantial enough to hit the world's headlines, be given names and endowed almost with personality.

But unlike other metals, gold is also to be found in salt water. Almost three-quarters of the earth's surface is covered by sea—an area of some 140,000,000 square miles in all; and though the percentage of gold in sea water never rises above 267 parts in every 100,000,000, nevertheless so vast is the total quantity of sea water in cubic miles that it has been calculated that it contains no less than 10,000,000,000 *tons* of gold!

This precious metal was certainly the first to be worked, and exploited, by man. It was well known to the Egyptians 8,000 years ago, and the Egyptians were but one civilization who mined and worked it. It appears in all the world's mythologies; it occurs in countless legends, fables and superstitions; it has played its part in many of the world's religions; it has helped to create, and later to destroy, communities great and small; it has bred feuds, vendettas and wars; it has been the essence of some of the most beautiful and lasting of all man's creative work, and has been responsible for some of the most ignoble of all his activities.

There is hardly a poet, philosopher, pedagogue, prelate or politician who has not recognized the inherent dual qualities of gold: its power to inspire and to corrupt man; to exalt him and degrade him. "Men dig the earth for gold," Ovid wrote, "seed of unnumber'd ills," and Samuel Johnson spoke of "The lust of gold, unfeeling and remorseless, the last corruption of degenerate man!"

9

In the nineteenth century Byron wrote of "A thirst for gold, the beggar's vice, which can but overwhelm the meanest hearts," and Shelley wrote of gold as "A living god who rules in scorn all earthly things but virtue." Two thousand years previously, Diogenes, who peremptorily ordered Alexander the Great to remove his shadow from the entrance to his barrel-home, observed that "Gold is pale because it has so many thieves plotting against it."

Gold inevitably found its way into the proverb, the colloquial epitome of accumulated folk-wisdom. "Gold dust blinds all eyes," says one of these; another says, "Gold goes in at any gate, except Heaven's," and yet another comes even nearer home with: "A fool and his gold are soon parted."

To take note of the innumerable references to gold down the ages is to realize that thinking man has become increasingly aware of one inescapable fact: gold brings more evil in its train than happiness; it debases more certainly than it truly enriches. "Gold," said the philosopher, Francis Bacon, "is tried with the touchstone, but men with gold!" And "Gold," said Senator Ingalls four hundred years later, "is the instrument of gamblers and speculators and the idol of the miser and the thief. It is the most cowardly and treacherous of all metals. It makes no treaty that it does not break; it makes no friend whom it does not sooner or later betray."

The story of gold, and its association with man, is infinitely varied. It sweeps across the hemispheres and through time, embracing every nation, every age. It takes in the Spanish Main and the Inner Hebrides, the Valley of the Kings and the mountain fastnesses of the High Andes, the Italian Renaissance and the Aztecs and Incas of Peru. It takes in the stage-coach hold-ups of the nineteenth century and the bullion robberies of the twentieth; the misers of history and fiction and the Carnegies and Rockefellers of our modern world; the gold rushes of yesterday and the gold-salvaging operations of today.

Croesus and Midas, King Solomon and the Queen of Sheba, Aesop's Golden Goose and Portia's Golden Casket, Hermes Trismegistus and the modern research chemist, the Israelites' Golden Calf and Jason's Golden Fleece and the Leprechaun's Crock of Gold: these are only a few of the facets of this precious metal that have gleamed alluringly throughout the long history of mankind.

Man's quest for gold—his lust for gold is the truer phrase—has been unceasing, his efforts indefatigable; but his use of it, so history suggests and all thoughtful writers confirm, has been less noticeable than his abundant and persistent misuse. "Gold," said Shakespeare, in whose plays the references are legion, "is poison to men's souls"; and again: " 'Tis gold which makes the true man kill'd and saves the thief." Pindar wrote, two thousand years earlier: "Gold is the Child of Zeus; neither moth nor rust devoureth it; but the mind of man is devoured by this supreme possession." And Thomas Hood, who had a knack of expressing in simple, direct verse ideas often more profound than they appeared, summed up the matter thus:

> "Gold! Gold! Gold! Gold!
> Bright and yellow, hard and cold,
> Molten, graven, hammered, rolled;
> Heavy to get and light to hold,
> Hoarded, bartered, squandered, doled,
> Price of many a crime untold:
> Gold! Gold! Gold! Gold!—
> Good or bad, a thousandfold!"

ONE

Gold in Myth and Legend

"Whereas Gold is the kindest of Hosts when it shines in the Sky, it
comes as an evil Guest unto those that receive it in their Hands."
Plutarch.

IN remotest times, when the world was yet young and mythology
was still in the making, man seems to have been aware not only of
the material value of gold but of its influence upon him. It was
understood to possess, Stein remarks, "a power that radiates out into
space, a power by which man himself would like to be carried away:
that is why he wants to take possession of gold. In earliest times man
felt that gold brings blessing because it contains Sun Powers within
itself. But if these cosmic, expansive powers of gold fall victim to
narrow egoism (or greed), then gold becomes a curse."

Desire for limitless wealth—particularly in the form of gold, which
man has always considered to be inextricably bound up with his
welfare—has brought misfortune or catastrophe to untold numbers
of men and women in history and legend; mythology has taken note
of the fact, and used it for its own purposes. The legend of Midas,
King of the Phrygians, is a classic and beautiful example: beautiful
because gold was literally thrust down the throat of one whose
avarice had overstepped the bounds of what the gods thought
proper. Ovid tells the story in Book XI of his *Metamorphoses*, and
the version that follows is from the pen of an anonymous translator
who turned it into English some seventy or eighty years ago:

Now Bacchus and his rout of Satyrs make for the vineyards of
Timolus, but Silenus, the god's foster-father, is absent. The rustic
Phrygians had seized him, tottering with age and the great
draughts of wine he had drunk, and dragged him, bound with
garlands, into the presence of King Midas. On the arrival of the
old man, the Phrygian king began a merry feast which he kept
for five days and as many nights. And now the eleventh dawn had
driven away the high host of stars, when King Midas comes in
joy to the vineyards and restores old Silenus to his foster-child.
Bacchus rejoices that his father has been restored to him, and

13

gives the king the choice of any wish that he might desire to have
fulfilled. He, being about to make not at all a good use of this
gift, says: "Let everything that I may touch with my person be
at once turned to purest gold." The god grants his wish, though
he is grieved that the king should not have named a better one.
"So shall it be hereafter," he says; and goes on his way.

Eager to put it to the test, King Midas thereupon proceeds to
lay his finger upon a green twig of holm-oak. Immediately, the
twig becomes golden! He lifts a rock from the ground at his feet,
and behold the rock, too, takes on the hue of purest gold! He
touches with his foot a clod of earth, and straightway it becomes
a golden mass! He plucks an ear or two of corn, and lo, the ears
are now gold! He picks an apple from a tree, and you would think
the apple had come straight from the Garden of the Hesperides!
He rests his hand against a lofty pillar, and at once it shines as
burnished gold from plinth to capital! He washes his hands in
clear water—and what then flows between his fingers would have
deceived Danäe!

He himself can scarcely contain the hopes that are aroused in
him, as he thinks that all he touches henceforth shall be turned to
purest gold. And while he is thus rejoicing, his servants are preparing a great feast, piling high his table with every variety of
delicacy such as he most loves to eat.

At last he approaches the sumptuous table and takes his
accustomed seat. He reaches out his hand for a luscious dish—
and behold, this gift of Ceres, Goddess of Plenty, becomes hard
even as he touches it! He prepares to close his teeth upon a dainty
morsel—and behold, it is now a yellow metal that lies hard
between his teeth! He takes up a goblet of rare wine, the very gift
of Bacchus himself—and behold, the tawny liquor becomes gold
on his palate and crowds his throat!

Astounded and dismayed at the extraordinary misfortune that
has befallen him, making him both wealthy and wretched at the
same moment, he now desperately longs to escape from his ill-
gotten riches and hates the object of his recent prayers. No
abundance can now relieve his hunger nor the dry thirst that now
parches his throat; he is deservedly tortured by the hated gold
that erstwhile he had so greatly coveted!

Raising his shining golden hands and arms aloft, he cries: "I
have sinned! Pity me! Rescue me from my woe, which once
looked like happiness!"

Kindly indeed is the divine nature of the gods. Bacchus restores the unhappy king to his former condition, now that he has confessed that he has sinned. "To prevent thyself from remaining clad in the gold of thy unhappy desire," he says to him, "go to the stream Pactolus and take thy way upstream against the gliding waters as they flow, until thou comest to the source of all its waters. There bend thy head beneath the foaming jet where it issues in fullest force, and so purge thy body and at the same time thy soul of its sin."

And King Midas does so. He goes beneath the waters as the god has bidden him. And now the gold passes from his body and dyes the stream, Pactolus. Moreover, the fields receive the seed of this golden water, and soon they shine on each bank of the stream with a golden hue, for all their soil is henceforward drenched with purest gold.

Gold was the downfall of Midas, King of Phrygia—or would have been, but for the timely intervention of Bacchus. Gold, too, was indirectly the cause of the ten-year-long Trojan War. Paris, handsome son of Priam, King of Troy, was in an unlucky moment invited by the gods to adjudicate in what is undoubtedly the earliest Beauty Contest on record; and also the most memorable. The competitors were themselves goddesses: Athene, Hera, and Aphrodite, better known, perhaps, as Venus. The prize to be awarded to the winner was a golden apple; with the irony which characterizes so many of these legends, it was the gift of Eris, Goddess of Strife! On the shining golden surface she had had inscribed the words: "For the Fairest". It was a title nicely calculated to engender the maximum degree of anger and bitterness in the hearts of the two losers.

Goddesses, being immortal, should have known better than to indulge in base subterfuge. But gold was the prize, as well as a title; and where gold is at stake, no underhand methods, no refinement of bribery and corruption, are too base to be adopted. Each of the goddesses, therefore, proceeded to offer lavish promises of reward: Hera promised him power and riches; Athene, wisdom and fame; Aphrodite, "The Fairest Woman in the World".

Now, Paris was already happily married to Oenone, and should have ignored that third bribe. Nevertheless, this was the bribe that won him over, and he accordingly awarded the golden apple to Aphrodite. It is to be hoped that his young wife, the fair Oenone, was not a spectator at the Beauty Contest!

Aphrodite was, of course, delighted with the result, and lost no time in fulfilling her promise. She contrived to bring young Paris into the presence of Helen, the beautiful wife of Menelaus, whose face, the poet tells us, "launched a thousand ships", and who was held to be the most beautiful mortal in the known world. Paris immediately forgot his wife, threw all caution to the winds, ignored the ancient and rigid laws of hospitality and the current rules of self-preservation, and persuaded Helen to elope with him. Thus was sparked-off the Trojan War.

The golden ball set mischief at work with a vengeance. King Priam's capital was besieged by the Greeks for ten years; Paris himself was mortally wounded by an arrow shot by Philoctetes and was graceless enough to seek comfort in the lap of his true wife whom he had so wantonly abandoned, which distressed her so much that after his death she committed suicide. Helen, with an eye to the main chance, married Paris's younger brother and enjoyed life with him until Troy ultimately fell to the Greeks, when she returned to Menelaus, who was magnanimous enough to take her back without too many questions asked. And Aphrodite, one imagines, amused herself by passing from hand to hand the golden ball she had so corruptly won ten years before, and turning over in her mind what further use she might make of it!

Gold, the pursuit of gold, the forms which gold assumed, the purposes to which gold might be put: all this obsessed those who lived in ancient, legendary times, just as it has obsessed those who, in historic times, have worked for it, exploited it, coveted it, sinned for it, used it and abused it. Man, today, takes a more practical view of it; to the ancients, however, it was a commodity prized above all others, but it was also an essence—something possessing a volition of its own. It possessed the power of self-increase; it could even, as the beautiful legend of Danäe illustrates, beget offspring.

Danäe was the lovely daughter of Acrisius, King of Argos. The king had heard a prophecy to the effect that he would be killed and his throne be seized by a son who would be born to his daughter. Determined to evade this calamity, he erected a brazen tower and immured his daughter within it, so that there should be no risk that anyone would see her beauty, fall in love with her and produce by her a son who might fulfil the oracle.

Acrisius, however, like many before and since his time, reckoned without the gods. Zeus himself, mightiest of the hierarchy of Greek gods and endowed with an insatiable love of experiment among not only the goddesses but the mortals below, had noted Danäe's outstanding beauty. A tower of brass was all that stood between him and his desires—a small matter, and one which was hardly worth his Olympian while to destroy. He therefore adopted a more subtle, and certainly more romantic method of effecting entry: he transformed himself into a shower of gold! This shower of gold duly impregnated Danäe, and the son born to her was none other than the mighty Perseus.

There is an odd twist to this story, one which shows how indirectly, in some instances, gold can have its effect on man. Terrified that the oracle would be fulfilled, since he had been outwitted once, Acrisius put his daughter and her infant son in a chest and set it afloat on the waves. The frail craft reached land; Perseus grew to manhood, and one day took part in an athletics contest at the funeral ceremony of the late King of Thessaly. One throw of his discus went wide, and struck a distinguished spectator in the grandstand. He was none other than Acrisius, his grandfather; who thus died at the hands of his daughter's son as the oracle had predicted!

The myth is a charming one; and like so many basic myths it is to be found in other mythologies. There is an almost exact parallel to it which concerns a certain Khan, or noble, of the Siberian Kirghiz. He had a daughter so beautiful that he was determined that no man should ever set eyes on her. He therefore locked her up in a dark cell while she was little more than a babe, and appointed a trustworthy woman to look after her.

One day, the story goes, when the child had grown to maidenhood, she asked the old woman why she went away from her every so often, and where she went.

"Into the bright world, where other people dwell," was the old woman's strange reply. The maiden begged and begged to be allowed, just once, to have a glimpse of this bright world, and finally the old woman in fear and trembling gave in.

But when the maiden left her dark cell and caught her first glimpse of the bright world outside, she fainted and fell to the ground. And there, says the legend, "the Eye of God rested on her, and she conceived."

In this legend, too, the father places his daughter, and the child so unexpectedly born to her, in a wooden chest, which he sets afloat on the chill waters.

Sir James Frazer, the great anthropologist, states that there is the closest parallel between the shower of gold in the Greek myth and the brilliant sunshine of the Kirghiz legend; and he adds that there is a widespread belief among many primitive tribes that a girl can be impregnated by the sun; and indeed many tribal wedding ceremonies involve a ritual in which sunlight plays a vital part.

Gold, and sunlight, are the dominant motif in the elaborate Icelandic and Scandinavian mythology known to us as the *Edda*, which dates back, if not so far as the mythology of the Greeks, yet at least a thousand years. The *Edda* tells of the three gods of Light, the Asen, who were continuously engaged in battle with the elements. They enlisted the support of the Giants, one of whom, Otter by name, was killed in battle. Thereupon, his brother giants turned on the Asen and demanded "death-gold" to compensate for his loss : it must be sufficient, they said, to make him a golden shroud and yet leave enough over to satisfy those who had survived him.

The Asen dispatched one of their number, Loki, to the banks of the Rhine, where he was to demand of Andvari, a dwarf who dwelt in a cave there, sufficient gold to satisfy the Giants. Andvari got word of the mission, and swiftly changed himself into a pike and dived into the deepest pool in the Rhine in the hope of avoiding discovery. Loki, however, successfully hooked him, brought him to the surface and demanded the gold. Andvari, knowing that he was no match for Loki, surrendered the gold, but made an attempt to secrete the gold ring, Andwarnaut, which possessed the magical gift of increasing indefinitely the wealth of anyone who owned it. Provided he could retain the ring, he would be able to replace the treasure which Loki was taking from him.

Loki was a match for Andvari in cunning, however, and threatened punishment so dire if the ring was not handed over that the dwarf gave in. But as he handed over the ring he uttered a solemn curse : "May everlasting misfortune dog the footsteps of him who takes from me this my golden ring!"

Quick as a flash, Loki retorted : "May your curse act only on him to whom I surrender this my golden ring!" And with that, he departed, leaving Andvari screaming maledictions upon him.

Now, when the shroud had been completed it was found that one strand of Otter's beard was not covered by the gold. His brother giants were enraged and Loki therefore laid the gold ring on the beard and secretly exulted in the thought that Andvari's curse should now be passing to another. And from that day onwards, says the *Edda*, gold became a curse that passed continuously from man to man, a curse that he would always seek and would only try to escape when it was too late.

With variants and elaborations, this Icelandic myth became absorbed in the Teutonic myth, the *Nibelungenlied*, a thirteenth-century heroic poem in which gold is the underlying motif, and its curse is disseminated among men and women, generation after generation. The Asen of the *Edda* have become the Anses: Odin, Loki and Hornir; the names of the Giants whose aid they enlisted are given. One of them is Rodmar; and it is he who seized for his own purposes the gold provided for the shroud of Otter.

But possession of the gold brought him no happiness and he was almost immediately slain by his two sons, Fafnir and Regin, who coveted the gold themselves. No sooner had they killed their father and made off with the gold than strife broke out between them: Fafnir, being the elder, demanding the whole of it for himself. In order to attain this end, he transformed himself into a serpent—the choice of creature is significant!—and retired to a desolate wilderness where he could lie beneath a great stone and gloat over his possessions. He is one of the earliest examples of the traditional miser.

Regin, having assisted his elder brother to slay their father, is naturally not content to lose his share of the gold, and he immediately sets about devising a way of achieving his revenge. The curse of the gold, laid upon it by Andvari and confirmed by Loki, is now well and truly in circulation!

In the *Nibelungenlied* the plot swiftly increases in complexity. Names change: Sigurd becoming Siegfried, for example. Sigurd is the warrior-swordsmith-apprentice who slays the serpent, Fafnir, and learns the language of the woodpeckers—who reveal to him that Regin is now plotting his destruction. Into the legend come Brünnhilde, the Valkyrie, and Gunnar, the Rhine prince whom she marries. But the ring of gold with the built-in curse is given to her as a betrothal ring, and thus the curse is transferred to her.

Gudrun comes into the swelling complexity of the tapestry when she marries Attila, King of the Huns; the *dramatis personae* of this story increases wildly, introducing a host of characters, including the magic steed, Grani; there is no foreseeable limit to a saga that is passed on by word of mouth from one to another during the long, dark evenings in the Europe of the Middle Ages.

The curse laid on the gold is disseminated more and more widely. Death and disaster overtake all those in whose possession it even temporarily remains. The Nibelungs must perish; and eventually the golden ring must find its way back to the spot on the bank of the Rhine where Andvari had guarded it until the fateful mission of Loki, the personification of avarice. So, the story comes full circle: the accursed golden ring had achieved its end.

Gold was considered by many ancient peoples—and indeed until comparatively modern times by the more simple communities—as the "Seed of Heaven": gold, and life-giving light and heat, were merely different aspects of the same basic principle. The Asen of the *Edda*, the Anses of the *Nibelungenlied*, existed in Indian mythology as the Asura, and in Persian mythology as Ahura Mazdao, the Ormuzd of the Zoroastrian religion who was the God of Light.

Primitive peoples, scattered as widely apart as Russia and Spain and including Tirolean peasants, the Swiss of the remoter districts, Bretons, Swedes and innumerable nomadic communities such as the Central European gypsies, believed until only yesterday in a manifestation of the life-giving principle of light-and-gold. They called it the "fern-seed", and this has often been identified with the parasitic mistletoe, the "golden bough" of many writers from Virgil to Sir James Frazer.

A man fortunate enough to come across a sprig of this plant on Midsummer Eve would be led up a mountain to buried gold; in Russia he need not even make the laborious journey up a mountain: all he had to do was to throw the twig into the air and it would soar like a shooting-star, to fall to earth immediately over the gold of his desire; in Sweden he must hold the twig as a dowser holds his divining-rod and it would begin to shiver as though it was alive, indicating unmistakably the point at which he should dig for buried gold. The emanations from the gold were believed to react upon the living plant, which itself was a "golden bough", so that its movements were an echo of the treasure lying hidden beneath it.

But what had given this life to the mistletoe? Why, the sun, of course: fire-and-gold in the heavens; and the mistletoe was living gold. The two were interfused. The mistletoe was "living fire" because it was the "golden bough", a manifestation of the sun, which gave it life. When a man kindled fire for himself by rubbing a pointed stick along a piece of grooved wood, taken very likely from a tree on which mistletoe grew, he was taking possession of a fragment of the fire that, he believed, dwelt in that tree and manifested itself in a bright cluster that shone like a glowing crown among its upper branches.

Such beliefs as these are, for us today, no more than somewhat absurd fantasies peopling the myriad pages of the world's mythologies; to our ancestors they were beliefs of vital importance, constituting the difference between life and death, part of the very essence of their being. The ramifications of the Sun-Life-Fire-Gold motif were labyrinthine; symbols were no less important to them than are our own fundamental beliefs today.

TWO

The Gold Makers

"You are an alchemist: make Gold of that!"
Shakespeare.

"For all oure craft, whenne we have all y-do,
With all oure sleighte, he will not come us to."
Chaucer.

In the whole span of recorded history there has never been a time
when there was sufficient gold to satisfy men's desires for it. Appetite
grew by what it fed on; gold must produce gold; the lives of a
thousand slaves toiling in Ethiopia and Nubia were expendable,
provided the coffers of the Pharaohs were enriched thereby.
Carvings and inscriptions show that the Egyptians mined gold
thousands of years B.C. It has been estimated that in the days of
Rameses II the annual production of gold was the equivalent of
£125,000,000 sterling. King Solomon obtained gold from the semi-
legendary mines of Ophir to a value of some £4,000,000 annually.
When the Queen of Sheba paid him a state visit she brought him
gold worth a million: nothing less was likely to interest him
particularly.

But even though gold was to be obtained in such quantities, they
were not sufficient, and men turned their inventive genius to methods
of producing the commodity which they lusted for by transmuting
baser metals. In China, Persia, Babylon, India, Arabia, Byzantium,
Morocco, Mesopotamia and Egypt, during the thirty centuries
preceding the Christian era, these alchemists, as they came to be
known, strove to wrest the secret from nature, to possess the
Philosopher's Stone which would work the transmutation for them
at will.

This Philosopher's Stone was also referred to as the Stone of the
Wise, as the *Magisterium*, as the Universal Essence; and in these
names there is implicit the conviction that the powers this long-
sought, mysterious agent possessed had the dual property of producing gold and also of giving health and prolonging life. It was
identified in the minds of the serious alchemists at least with the

21

long-sought Elixir of Life, a potion which was a fragment of the
Philosopher's Stone in liquid form.

Gold—and life: what had been myth and superstition became
religion. The practice of alchemy was closely bound up with
ritualistic practice; an alchemist worked in the greatest secrecy.
He spent his days on the point of discovering the ultimate secret:
when he succeeded, the world would become his oyster; and the
pearl in that oyster would be a million million times more valuable
than the finest known pearl, for it would mean the source of
unlimited wealth. Kings and princes and potentates would be
waiting on his doorstep; empires would stand or fall at his word!

A Chinese alchemist claimed to have evolved an Elixir of Life of
supreme potency. It was a divine elixir, produced only after he had
fasted for a hundred days. Its ingredients included sulphur and
cinnabar, oyster-shells and alum, red and yellow sulphide of arsenic,
mica, chalk and resin. Introduce this mixture to mercury, the
Chinese alchemist said, and the finest gold would be the happy
result.

Among the world's most patient and enterprising alchemists were
the Arabs—from whom the very word is derived. One of them,
Jabir ibn Hayyan, official alchemist to the Court of Haroun al
Raschid, was an innovator and experimentalist of note. He turned
for the ingredients that were to constitute his Philosopher's Stone
to the animal and vegetable worlds. Jasmine, pepper, mustard,
olives, ginger, onion and aconite were mingled with marrow,
crushed bones, hair, blood and urine from gazelles, vipers, donkeys
and even, when available, lions.

The principles of alchemy were imparted by the Arabs to Euro-
peans, and the art of alchemy reached its zenith in Europe in the
Middle Ages. One of the best known of the European alchemists
is a somewhat elusive figure, once possibly a Benedictine monk,
usually known as Basil Valentine. He published a number of
scientific treatises, one of which he entitled *The Great Stone of the
Philosophers*; it offers possibly the clearest exposition of what the
alchemists sought and found, and of the reasons for their search,
of all those that survive.

Take [he wrote] of the very best gold you can have, One Part;
and of good Hungarian antimony, Six Parts. Melt these together
upon a fire and pour it out into such a pot as the goldsmiths use.
It then becomes a Regulus. This Regulus is to be again melted,
and the antimony separated from it. Then add mercury, and

melt it again. Do this three times. Then beat the gold very thin, and make an amalgam with more quicksilver. Let the quicksilver fume away over a gentle fire till nothing remain but gold. Then take One Part of saltpetre and One Part of sal ammoniac and half as much of pebbles well washed. Mix them, and distill in an earthen retort in a furnace.

The fluid is then mixed with the prepared calx of gold, and water added. Digest it in warm ashes at a gentle heat for Fourteen Days. Add water again, distill and redistill until the gold comes over. To this spiritualized solution of gold, rain water is added, and Three Parts of mercury. Decant the water and dry the amalgam, drive off the quicksilver, and there will remain a very fair powder, of a purple colour. Then must be made the Tartar of the Philosophers from the ashes of the vine and make a strong lee with it to coagulation. There remains a reddish matter, which must be dissolved in spirit of wine. Then take the other part of mercury of pure gold and pour on and distill. The precipitated mercury and the oyl of gold are then to be mixed, placed in a hermetically sealed glass and put into a threefold furnace and allowed to putrefy for a month and become quite black.

Increase the fire, and the blackness will vanish. It changes to many colours. Increase it to the fourth degree, and the glass will look like silver; to the fifth degree, and it becomes like gold. Continue this, and you will see your Matter lye beneath like a brown oyl, which at length becomes dry like granite.

He that obtains this, may render thanks to God, for poverty will forsake him; for this noble medicine is such a Stone to which nothing in the world may be compared for virtue, riches and power. If this medicine, after being fermented with other pure gold, doth likewise tinge many thousand parts of all other metals into very good gold, such gold likewise becometh a penetrate medicine, that one part thereof will transmute a thousand parts of other metals, and much more beyond belief, into perfect gold.

Philosophers' Stones seem to have differed substantially in appearance—which is perhaps not entirely surprising in view of the infinite number of recipes recommended for its creation! Perhaps it should not really be looked upon as a stone at all, but as something more tractable. One alchemist described it as follows: "Its appearance is that of a very fine powder, impalpable to the touch, sweet to the taste, fragrant to the smell; in potency a most penetrative spirit, apparently dry and yet unctuous and easily capable of

tingeing a plate of metal." Another alchemist, Paracelsus, described it as being "solid like a ruby, yet transparent and flexible".
It has been variously described as yellow, the colour of saffron,
brilliant as glass, bluish-grey or greyish-green, the colour of a wild
poppy, sable with intermixed argent.

It varied greatly, too, in its powers. Roger Bacon claimed that
it was capable of transmuting one hundred thousand times its
weight; a Dutch alchemist went so far as to estimate its powers at
a millionfold. Daustein, a medieval alchemist, wrote to Pope
John XXII:

> One part converts a million parts of any body you may choose
> into the most genuine gold. The Elixir has effective virtue over
> all other medicines, to cure all infirmities. If an infirmity of one
> month, it cures within one day; if it be an illness of a year, then
> in twelve days; if it be an inveterate illness, then in one month.
> This *Magisterium* is for Kings and the Greate of this Worlde. He
> who possesses it, has a never-failing Treasure.

Comparatively few of these dabblers in jasmine and sal ammoniac,
chalk, resin and the blood and urine of lions and gazelles, were on
letter-writing terms with the Popes. The majority of them, in fact,
were charlatans; at least in medieval Europe. Mystery surrounded
their birth, their activities, their whereabouts; they tended to be
nomadic: popping up here and there, to astonish or, more often,
disappoint, and vanishing overnight to the sound of gnashing teeth
and murderous threats from those they had duped. Their travel
warrants derived from the eternal gullibility of those whose ambition
was easy money.

It is not only today that a fool is born every minute. In the Middle
Ages, too, there were always men easy enough to dupe with tales
of gold. The fair-ground thimble-riggers, the confidence-tricksters
with their stories of lost gold mines only awaiting discovery, their
evidence of "solid" gold bricks, are the descendants of the nimble-
witted quack alchemists who threaded their profitable way among
the towns and cities of a gullible Europe five, six and seven hundred
years ago.

There were as many ways of duping a small, hand-picked
audience as there were charlatans. The bogus alchemist looked first
for a man of substance—a merchant, a priest, a noble. He let him
know that, if he was prepared to give him audience, he might hear
something to his advantage. He equipped himself with certain stage

properties: a crucible; some mercury; variously coloured powders; a phial or two of coloured liquid; a variety of rods made of glass or metal polished to resemble silver; a capsule or two which were much in evidence but never opened. Enough, in fact, to arouse curiosity.

One of the simplest and most consistently effective tricks was the unobtrusive insertion of a fragment of genuine gold into the contents of the crucible. Sometimes a cube of charcoal would be hollowed out in advance and the gold inserted into it; sometimes a hollow rod containing a fragment of gold sealed into it with wax would be used. The heat of the ingredients in the crucible would release the gold— which the spectators would have been prepared to swear was not among those ingredients when the experiment began.

The rest was easy. An assayer would attest to the purity of the gold; the merchant would respond swiftly to the suggestion that funds should be forthcoming for the purchase of base metals and other ingredients which, together, would repeat the happy experiment on a much more satisfactory scale; and the charlatan would abscond overnight with the money that had been handed over to him! Alternatively, he would sell to the merchant a very small quantity of his precious Philosopher's Stone, which he had allegedly taken from one of those sealed capsules, leaving the merchant the poorer by a substantial sum which he had handed over in exchange for some worthless flakes of common rock or some coloured powder. By the time he had realized how he had been duped, the glib alchemist would have put many leagues between himself and the scene of his trickery.

Occasionally one of these virtuosi of charlatanry would operate on the grand scale. For example, there appeared in Prague one fine day a man wearing the dress of an Arab of high degree. A retinue of Arab servants attended him, and on his behalf one of them put down a considerable sum of money for the use of a great house in the best part of the city. Tradesmen reported that nothing but the best was good enough for him, whether in food, drink, apparel or entertainment. It was not long before the *élite* of Prague were doing their very best to obtain introductions to him: which was exactly what he had hoped they would do.

In due course he announced that he proposed to hold a banquet at his house which would be followed by a demonstration of the art of the alchemist compared with which all such demonstrations in Prague, at that time the centre of alchemy in Europe, would seem no more than foolish child's play. In one sense, this was not to be a

free banquet: it was open to any of the Prague nobility who were
prepared to bring with them very considerable sums of gold. But
he guaranteed that he would multiply such sums of gold by ten
times at least. For every hundred marks a guest brought with him,
he would depart at midnight with not less than a thousand.

It was indeed a magnificent banquet. The dishes followed one
another endlessly, each more sumptuous than the last, and every
new bottle that was opened proved to contain liquor more delectable
than the one that had preceded it. The host, wearing his oriental
robes and a turban in which fabulous jewels sparkled in the light
of a thousand torches, presided amiably—which was hardly
surprising in view of the fact that as each guest arrived he had
handed over to one of his servants a sum of gold often running to
many hundreds of pounds!

The time came for the guests to follow their host into his
laboratory. It was more elaborately equipped than any they had
ever seen before. In one corner a great furnace blazed, whipped to
white heat by an Arab sweating at the bellows. There were racks
and benches covered with all the paraphernalia of the alchemist:
stills, alembics, crucibles, mortars and pestles, aludels and sublima-
tories, athanors, cucurbits, serpent-condensers, kerotakides, braziers,
cupellas, matrasses, pelicans; and hour- and minute-glasses for
timing individual stages of the experiments carried on there. The
guests were dumbfounded at what they saw.

The procedure adopted by the Arab alchemist was as simple as
his apparatus was elaborate. He motioned to his assistant to remove
the lid of the crucible, which was glowing red-hot on the charcoal,
and into it he appeared to pour the gold which his guests had
previously handed over. To this, with a merry quip about seeing no
reason why he should not augment some of his own gold, he added
another handful or two. Then, with the appropriate air of mystery
that was an essential part of any alchemist's stock-in-trade, he took
some mercury from one container, some salt, some *aqua fortis*, some
lead and some copperas from other containers, weighed them
carefully and in full view of his guests, and tipped all this into the
crucible. Then he bade the attendant apply himself with renewed
vigour to the bellows.

His guests crowded round the furnace in a tight semi-circle,
hardly able to contain their eagerness. The crucible changed from
red hot to orange hot, to ivory hot, to white hot as the assistant
swung at the bellows. He, and only he, saw the prearranged
unobtrusive signal his master gave. There was a sudden tremendous

explosion. The red-hot coals and fragments of white-hot crucible were blasted from the heart of the furnace and sprayed across the laboratory, searing the eager faces and filling the whole room with fumes so poisonous and suffocating that even those who had escaped injury from the burning coals were overwhelmed and fell unconscious to the smooth tiled floor.

Shrieks of agony filled the now murky air, lit only by the lurid glare of the flames from the few coals still in the furnace. When the least badly injured guests at last struggled to their feet and felt their way across the floor, their host and his assistants had departed. And with them, they now realized in an agony as much mental as physical, they had taken the gold they had so unsuspectingly handed over on arriving for the banquet in the hope of a tenfold increase. Though Prague at their orders was searched as with a fine tooth-comb, the bogus Arab and his retinue had softly and silently faded away, never to be seen again!

This was a classic example of skilful charlatanry. One might be inclined to say that it could have succeeded only in an age when people were less sophisticated than they are today. But this would be to overlook the tremendously powerful influence that the expectation of gold can exert over men.

At the turn of last century an American boldly announced that after half a lifetime's search he had at last succeeded in producing the Philosopher's Stone. His claims for it were modest by the standard of the Middle Ages: it did not contain the Elixir of Life; it would not transmute base metals such as lead into pure gold; it would not even multiply a given quantity of gold a hundred, or even ten times. But it positively would, he asserted, multiply any given weight of gold three times over. That claim was quite sufficient to get people interested.

He played his cards cannily. These things, he explained with a guileless air, took time. A period of eighteen days must be allowed to elapse between the firing of the crucible with its contents of gold and the secret Stone and other ingredients, and the removal of those contents, increased to three times their original value. He admitted that such a condition must make him suspect. Very well, then: he would conduct his experiment behind locked doors; the keys should be held by those who entrusted their gold to him; and as an added guarantee of his integrity he would like to have the doors sealed. He added, for good measure, that since the ingredients that he would place in the crucible produced noxious fumes, he would have all apertures of door frames and windows hermetically sealed, and no one would set foot within the room until the eighteenth day.

Incredible as it may seem, he persuaded a number of sponsors to let him have a total of 100,000 dollars in gold, with the proviso that they would all receive three times the amount of their loan when the locked room was opened. The fire was lit, the crucible was filled and the lid placed over it. The room was locked, the doors and windows hermetically sealed; only the long wooden arm of a bellows projected from the wall, to be kept in motion by a succession of labourers until the end of the first day, by which time heat would have broken down the ingredients and the fluid in the crucible would begin its magical work.

At the end of the eighteen days, the sponsors met by agreement to watch the unsealing of the room and the opening of the crucible into which they had poured their 100,000 gold dollars. The alchemist, however, was not there to greet them. They noticed that the seals had been broken. Also, that though they possessed what they believed to be the only keys, in fact the door was unlocked! They burst into the room. And found—as they might have known, had they not been so blinded by the expectation of easy money— that the crucible contained no more than a slight discoloration at the bottom. There was not even any smell to it. As for the gold with which they had entrusted their fellow-countryman: they had wit enough to know that they would never see that again, let alone the threefold bonus they had so naïvely anticipated!

The late twenties and early thirties of this century, the years of the Great Depression that lay like a cloud over much of Europe and America, were notable for some large-scale exploitation of the get-rich-quick instinct. Among the most successful of these exploiters was a German named Franz Tausend—his name alone was worth something to him in his particular line of charlatanry! He cashed-in on the swiftly rising tide of popular scientific knowledge. He read enough to be able to talk fluently and facilely of atomic and molecular structure in metals, of the power of great heat to break down structures and reassemble them in different forms. He amassed a fine-sounding catalogue of formulae, which rolled easily off his tongue; and he had a happy knack of meeting the right people at the right moment. You would never have believed that he had been, until a short time before, a plumber.

Aware that it is the man in the smart suit, with the good car, who impresses, Tausend contrived so to equip himself. He got himself talked about. He raised sufficient funds to fit out a small laboratory.

He fitted out also a compact travelling outfit with which he appeared here and there in Europe to give spectacular demonstrations of a kind likely to impress the credulous who did not trouble to look beneath the superficial results.

During this stage in his campaign he skilfully kept his various contacts as it were in watertight compartments. Someone here, someone there, someone else, each believed that he alone was the happy recipient of a fragment of genuine gold which, in the course of a demonstration, had been produced in one of the pieces of chemical equipment. It was pleasant to slip one's fingers into the corner of a waistcoat pocket and immediately find tangible evidence of one's good sense in placing confidence in an obviously gifted man; reassuring to know that a reputable assayer had verified the purity of the gold!

When the time was ripe, Franz Tausend suggested that those who had benefited from his laboratory work should organize themselves into a society. It should be a highly exclusive society, limited in fact to no more than thirty members. But each of these was hand-picked on the basis of his monetary resources. The object of the society was the enrichment of the members on a scale hitherto not attempted: gold begets gold, was Tausend's thesis, and the members' firm credo. They called themselves "The 164 Society", the figure being a key one in Tausend's grandiose-sounding "Vibrational Theory of Atomic and Molecular Structure".

It is surprising that so many as thirty individuals, all of them closely connected with the business world and accustomed to the handling of money, should be so foolish as to lay themselves wide open to the obvious risk of large-scale swindling. The explanation lies in Tausend's astuteness: he made a point of paying interim dividends substantial enough to allay any possible suspicion. They were not large, and they were not regular; but they were enough to keep a handful of covetous men interested: an occasional knob of gold, produced (they assumed) in the laboratory which they had largely financed and into which they had poured an initial sum of gold designed to beget much greater sums, was bait enough to keep them on the hook. They unquestioningly accepted Tausend's promise that when his laboratory was in full production it would be showing a steady return of some £5,000 in gold every month. In time, there would be, he said, gold *by the ton*. Given a modicum of patience, the sky was the limit. . . .

It may have been; but it must be said that the cloud-ceiling was very low. The first suspicions were aroused when it was found that

Tausend had acquired a country property some distance from his base and was living in a style that argued that a good deal of money had been transferred to purposes other than those of multiplying gold in the crucible. Members of The 164 Society became restive. They engaged a discreet detective, and as a result of his report, called for a meeting of the shareholders. Tausend found the atmosphere of the meeting very different from that of earlier meetings, and became uneasy. He decided that he had better leave, and without delay.

The shareholders, however, had foreseen that possible reaction, and Franz Tausend stepped straight into the hands of the police who had in the meantime been instructed to surround the building. Subsequent investigation revealed that he had netted about £100,000 clear during this relatively short spell of exploiting human cupidity. The years he subsequently spent in gaol offered him the opportunity to consider how very much better off, in fact, he might have been had he stayed with his father and eventually succeeded to the business. Lead, on all counts, is a safer metal with which to work than garish gold.

It is, perhaps, unfair to dismiss the whole subject of alchemy, in so far as it concerns the transmutation of base metals into gold, or the multiplying of gold by application of the Philosopher's Stone, as no more than a remarkably well sustained piece of bluff, a protracted exploitation of the basic instinct of avarice. Though it has not yet been conclusively proved that any alchemist did, in fact, succeed in making gold, there are cases which are singularly hard to disprove. That, for example, of Helvetius.

Helvetius was a Swiss named Johann Friedrich Schweitzer, a qualified doctor and Court Physician to the Prince of Orange. He was the author of a considerable number of medical and botanical works which bear all the marks of a cultured, sober, intelligent and philosophic mind. Contained in one of his books is a factual and for the most part impartial and unemotional account of his first contact with an alchemist and his own conversion to the art and practice of alchemy. This account has been well known for some three hundred years; it has been analysed and probed by successive generations of sceptics; but no loophole has ever been discovered in it. It bears every evidence of authenticity and verisimilitude.

On the 27th of December, 1666, [he wrote] in the afternoon, came a Stranger to my house, in a plebeian habit, honest Gravity, and serious Authority; of a mean Stature, a little long face with a few small pock holes, most black hair, a beardless chin, about three or four and forty years of age, as I guessed. He told me he had read some of my treatises, and asked me if I could not believe that such a medicine was in Nature as could cure all diseases. To which I replied that I had never seen such a medicine, though I had read much of it. He then told me that he had learned many rare things and asked if I should know the Philosopher's Stone if I should see it.

As I pondered my reply, he took out of his bosom pocket a neat ivory box, and out of that, three ponderous small lumps of the Stone, each about the bigness of a small walnut, transparent, of a pale brimstone colour, wherunto did stick the internal scales of the crucible wherein this most noble substance had been melted. The value of these, he told me, was to be judged as twenty tons of gold.

I returned to him this treasure of treasures, truly with a most sorrowful mind, after the custom of those who conquer themselves, yet (as was but just) very humbly. I requested him to bestow a little piece on me, though it were no more than the quantity of a coriander seed. And at last he gave me a crumb as big as a rape seed, saying: "Receive this small parcel of the greatest treasure of the world, which truly few Kings or Princes have ever seen. Put into thy crucible no more Lead than this can work upon, and it will transmute it into Gold."

Helvetius then describes how his unknown visitor takes his leave, and during the next few days he begins to doubt whether in fact he ever received such a visit. But his wife, to whom he had mentioned the matter, continuously nagged at him to put the gift to the test.

So [he goes on] I commanded a fire to be made. I then cut some grammes of old Lead and put them into the crucible in the fire. Then I put in my Treasure, which I had made up into a small pill. And presently there was such a hissing and bubbling as I had never heard. And within a quarter of an hour all that mass of Lead was totally transmuted into the finest Gold, which made us all amazed as though planet-struck. I could not sufficiently gaze upon this so admirable a work of Nature; for this melted Lead showed us the rarest and most beautiful colours imaginable; yea, and the greenest colour, as soon as I poured forth into an ingot, took on the lively fresh colour of blood; and being cold, shined as the purest and most refined transplendent Gold. A goldsmith, after a short trial, judged it the most excellent Gold in the whole world and offered to give most willingly fifty florins for every ounce of it.

It is a curious tale. The Stranger in plebeian habit and of serious Authority, the little, long face and beardless chin, never returned. Was he, the good Swiss doctor wondered, a man with a mission: dedicated to the conversion of the intelligent sceptic by ocular demonstrations of his art, but given to vanishing afterwards, leaving the convert to develop his own skill, handing on the torch of alchemy for his successors to tend? Or was Helvetius himself, for all his intelligence and scepticism, the dupe of yet another example of sleight-of-hand? It hardly seems possible that this should be so; and the manner in which he tells his story begets confidence. The facts have never been disproved. Even if his story is taken as no more than a seventeenth-century fable, nevertheless it contains a germ that has puzzled investigators and scientists ever since; and leaves even the most hard-bitten sceptic with an uneasy question-mark in his mind.

THREE

Gold Seekers

"In a cavern, in a canyon,
Excavating for a mine,
Dwelt a miner, 'Forty-niner . . ."
Traditional.

In a sense, the Spaniards who, following Columbus, rifled the hills
and valleys of Central and Southern America, press-ganged the
Peruvians to work for them, and even brought over miners from
Spain to exploit the gold deposits that the unhappy Incas and
Chibchas revealed to them, were the first to take part in a "gold
rush". But the first gold rush in the accepted sense is that in which
the gentleman of the verse at the head of this chapter took part—
together, possibly, with his heavy-footed daughter and most certainly
with some scores, even hundreds, of thousands of other prospectors
in 1849. This fantastic episode in American history was the result
of pure chance.

In the winter of 1847–8 a Swiss immigrant invited a New Jersey
contractor to build him a sawmill on his estate that bordered a
tributary of the Sacramento River. While constructing the tail-race
that would carry the water back to the main stream after it had
operated the water-wheel, the contractor happened to notice something glinting in the gravel over which the water ran. He dropped
to his knees to investigate more closely, and found that the rough
planking he had laid down had already begun to be covered with
fine silt. The lighter particles of silt were in continuous motion;
but the heavier ones lay still, trapped by the rough surface. And
what is more: they possessed a sheen which was quite unmistakable.

He was in a difficult situation. The temptation to keep his secret
to himself was great: if there was gold dust in the district proportionate to the deposit that had already built up on his planking,
then he was on to a good thing; on the other hand, this was his
employer's territory, and he could hardly hope to exploit it without
discovery. Later in the half-century of the great gold rushes,
when the powerful influence of the precious metal had led men to
indulge their basest instincts in order to satisfy their lust for gold,

he might have acted differently. But he was still only on the threshold of events, and acted honourably. He told his employer what he had discovered, and his response was as generous as his own gesture had been: henceforward they would be partners, splitting the proceeds fifty-fifty.

But the inevitable happened. Others got wind of what was afoot; before very long the spearhead of what proved to be a swarm of many thousands of men thrust its way into this corner of the Sacramento Valley. Their advent can only be compared with that of a swarm of locusts. The Swiss landowner's property became their hunting-ground and, worse still, their source of raw materials. His trees were uprooted or felled for timber baulks; his buildings were requisitioned for sleeping-quarters, or demolished and carried up the valley piecemeal, to provide planking, roofing, temporary structures of many kinds. His cattle were ruthlessly slaughtered for food. Mining claims were staked out in all likely and unlikely spots on his estate and on the river bank which skirted it. Sluices were built from his own timber, to channel off water for individual panning. Sutter, the owner, and Marshall, the builder who became his partner, were helpless in face of the ever-growing hordes of prospectors who poured in upon them; to protest without a show of force was futile; to show fight was to invite the raising of shotguns to the shoulder and threats of violence which clearly were no empty threats. Sutter lost everything he owned and became virtually a prisoner on his own estate, with eviction the only alternative. It was the first, but by no means the last, illustration of what takes hold of men when gold fever runs in their veins.

Those first invaders of the Sacramento Valley were tapping virgin soil, and were successful beyond their wildest hopes. They arrived in their thousands and, in the early months at least, picked up gold at every turn. Exuberant at their success, they broke off now and then to make whoopee in San Francisco and Monterey, smacking down on saloon bar counters their tins and buckskin wallets of pure gold dust and drinking themselves under the tables in the sawdust on the floor. They had left behind them, for a glorious day and night or two of unprecedented spending and drinking, the "strikes" they had named El Dorado, Jackass Hill, Rough-and-Ready, Angels' Camp, Sailors' Slide and Fiddletown— hut settlements hurriedly thrown together and lacking all amenities; and it was from such strikes as these that the gold dust flowed which brought wealth to San Francisco and Monterey and established the foundations on which the immensely prosperous

State of California was built, and from which it grew to its present position of affluence and importance.

And who were the men who constituted this vast army of gold seekers? Before the end of 1849 there were not far short of 100,000 of them: trappers and miners, farmers and hired men, doctors, druggists, lawyers, soldiers and sailors, preachers and school-teachers. . . .

> "Gold! We leap from our benches;
> Gold! We spring from our stools;
> Gold! We whirled in the furrow, fired with the faith of fools:
> Fearless, unfound, unfitted, far from the night and cold,
> Heard we the clarion summons, followed the master-lure:
> GOLD!"

. . . Robert W. Service caught the spirit of '49, as of so much else, in his *Rough Rhymes*. There were Americans, of course, from every corner of the continent; there were Chinese and Kanakas, Malays, British, French, Germans. They came by sea, across the prairies in their "prairie-schooners", along the Mormons' route of '46 by way of Salt Lake City and the notorious Oregon Trail of '42. They braved the fearsome Colorado Desert, the unpredictable Indian tribes, the headwaters of the Humboldt River and the slopes of the mighty Sierra Nevada, some of which were so steep that they had to sling their wagons in great rope and leather slings and lower them bodily over precipices. They came in small groups and organized parties of a hundred or more, taking many months over the journey, with no absolute certainly that they would ever arrive, or that there would be anything left for them if they did arrive. Such was the magnetic power of the sheer rumour of gold.

In those pioneering gold-rush days there was only one principle, but it was accepted by all: Every man for himself. Every man, too, was a law unto himself—and mob law was only just round the corner; justice, when it was in evidence at all, was summary and swift. Gould Buffum, in a book he titled *Six Months in the Gold Mines* and published in 1850, describes how it was put into practice:

Two Frenchmen and a Chilean were caught in the act of robbing another miner of his hard-earned gold dust. They were first brutally flogged by a group of fellow miners and then removed to a neighbouring shed where, because they were so weak from their punishment, they were laid stretched on the floor. They were then tried, in their absence, by a crowd of some 200 men, who had organized themselves into a jury and appointed a judge. The general sentiment was that they ought to be got rid of. At the close of the trial, which lasted 30 minutes, the judge put it to the vote. A universal affirmative was the response, and when the question of the punishment to be inflicted was raised, a brutal-looking fellow cried out, "Hang them!"

The proposition met with almost universal approbation. I mounted a stump and in the name of God, humanity and law, protested. But the crowd, by this time excited by frequent and deep potations of liquor, would listen to nothing contrary to their brutal desires, and even threatened to hang me too, if I did not immediately desist.

Thirty minutes only were allowed the unhappy victims to prepare themselves. Then, three ropes were attached to a limb of a tree. The prisoners were placed on a wagon and the ropes put round their necks. They vainly tried to speak, but none of them understanding English, they were obliged to use their native tongues. Vainly they called for an interpreter, but their cries were drowned by the yells of the now infuriated mob. A black handkerchief was bound around the eyes of each; their arms were pinioned, and at a given signal, without priest or prayer-book, the wagon was drawn from under them and they were launched into eternity.

It is not difficult to see why there was this intense feeling against gold pickpockets. The gold was won by the most laborious methods, and every grain was a prize. The average haul per man in those Californian gold-fields was barely half an ounce per day—a microscopic quantity which, if it were of almost any other commodity, would not be worth the picking up, let alone pickpocketing. But some idea of the numbers engaged in seeking gold in that first fabulous year may be obtained when it is realized that some 2,500,000 ounces of gold dust passed through the buyers' and dealers' hands in twelve months; and this figure does not take into account the gold which the individual miners handled and negotiated in other ways.

Their precious dust was won mainly by "pan" and "rocker". The first item was not unlike a common frying-pan with a flat base a foot or so in diameter and sloping sides four or five inches high. Into it, a shovelful of silt, mud or earth or fine gravel, mixed with water, was tipped. The panner kept his pan moving with a semi-

rotary motion, the effect of which was to let the finer grains of silt
wash over its sides while the heavier grains, of gold (if any), sank
to the bottom. A lucky strike might mean that a few of these
grains appeared in every other shovelful; an unlucky strike
might mean a day's panning without a grain of gold to show for it.
The half-ounce per day was an average only.

From the pan the rocker developed. It consisted of a rough
wooden box (even, sometimes, of a hollowed-out log) a yard long,
two feet wide and four or five inches deep. One end was open, the
other fitted with a sieve, or grid. On the bottom of the box a
number of light battens, or "riffles", were nailed across its width.
Finally, a pair of curved slats, taken maybe from a broken-up barrel,
were fitted underneath so that the whole contraption could be
rocked like a baby's cradle.

This was used by two- or three-man units; one man shovelled the
earth, silt or mud in at the open end, another kept it rocking and
the third scanned the "riffles" designed to trap the heavier gold
particles while the lighter silt flowed past to the exit. A rocker was
more profitable than the individual pan, provided there was
adequate water to flow through it; the average daily haul from it
was considerably greater; but it had, of course, to be divided among
the three partners. It might work out at an average of an ounce
per head. With gold running at between five and ten dollars the
ounce, according to the honesty of the buyer and persuasiveness of
the miner, it was well worth organizing three-man units and fitting
out a "gold-rocker".

Less than ten years later came the second great gold rush, this
time to Colorado. Rumours were heard that the Cherokee Indians
in the Arkansas River region had struck gold in quantity. By then,
the Californian gold-fields had been for the most part gutted: there
were miners on the look-out for a change of scene.

If the '49 gold rush had illustrated the effects of the lust for gold
on the individual gold seeker, its successor was to illustrate the
wiles of the bogus promoter, the large-scale confidence-trickster, as
never before: the man who made the money—and he made it in
great quantities—was the man who virtually never put his foot
outside his own front door.

For the truth is that the much-advertised finds of gold in the
mountainous region known as Pike's Peak were almost entirely
spurious. One of the first to prospect in the area published his views
for all to read: "This thing," he said, "is being done by speculators
in town property out here and on the Colorado border and should

be denied by all the papers. Gold was never found in lumps such as
these that are being openly exhibited—not within 1,000 miles of
Pike's Peak. These men, the originators of such stories, designed
solely to advance their own interests, should be lynched. Let the
next lot of emigrants do this thing! Let any who may be thinking of
coming out be assured that they will curse the day they set forth!"

The speculators referred to were real-estate men in the small
Mississippi and Missouri townships through which the prospectors
would have to pass, and the shopkeepers in those towns. By whipping
up excitement, they might hope to channel untold numbers of
strangers through their streets; they would have to buy from their
shops, spend their money in their saloons, possibly settle down there
when they had found out the truth about Pike's Peak and felt too
humiliated (as well as too impoverished) to return to their homes.

Bogus strikes were continually reported; wallets of gold dust were
displayed before those most likely to have their appetites whetted;
free "official guides" were distributed in the streets of many towns,
among the passengers in the crowded river-boats; advertisements
appeared in newspapers hundreds of miles from Colorado, alluringly
worded. "Gold," said one of them, "exists throughout the Pike's
Peak region. It can be picked up anywhere—on the plains, in the
mountains, and by the streams. There is no end to the precious
metal. Nature herself would seem to have turned into a most
successful alchemist in converting the very sands of the streams into
gold." (The advertiser, perhaps, had been reading the story of
Midas and the stream, Pactolus!)

It is small wonder that a single voice crying in the wilderness
failed to make headway against such blandishments. The roads
through Mississippi and Missouri westwards into Colorado were
flooded with wagons, hand-carts, mules, barrows and individuals
humping loads on their backs, all heading for Pike's Peak. Something like 100,000 gold seekers passed through the townships in
which the speculators operated. Hardly a quarter of these, however,
reached their objective; and of those who did, only a handful had
the staying-power to work out the few tiny pockets of gold that did,
in fact, exist. It has been estimated that less than 1,000,000 dollars-
worth of gold in all was won. "We have toiled," reported one disillusioned gold seeker, "from sun-up to sun-down without winning
enough gold to pay for the sharpening of our picks."

In spite of such reports, the flood westwards swelled all the time.
They came by river-boat to the nearest navigable point, and then
took to the roads and trails and tracks; they came by prairie-

schooner, on horseback, muleback and on foot; they carried banners with slogans scrawled on them calculated to provide encouragement: "Pike's Peak—or Bust!" they read; and far more often than not, it was "Bust".

These so-called prairie-schooners were extraordinary vehicles: great wagons strengthened and adapted to the exacting demands of the westward trail. Solid shelves were built out over the wheels to serve as beds; cupboards were built into them; tough hickory hoops were bent and fitted into iron slots to carry a heavy canvas hood; springs were reinforced, harness duplicated; axles braced. For these were to become mobile homes, often for a party of six or more, and a formidably heavy cargo of equipment and provisions.

One of the published guide-books available for prospective gold seekers set down a catalogue of what was necessary for such a journey: 1,000 lbs. flour, 400 lbs. bacon, 200 lbs. sugar, 150 lbs. beans, 100 lbs. dried beef, 50 lbs. salt, 50 lbs. coffee, 40 lbs. dried fruit, 30 lbs. rice, 4 gals. vinegar, 50 lbs. lead for bullets, 1,000 gun caps. In addition: plates, knives, spoons, pans, pots, a "Dutch" oven; picks, shovels, axes, augers, hammers, nails, rope, chain and tackle; blankets, rugs, sheeting, canvas, bedding and miscellaneous. The prairie-schooners had to carry such loads, plus their occupants, over such trails as the Santa Fé, the Oregon and the Overland; but also over open prairie devoid of trails, through rivers, up and down steep mountains, through swamps. It is small wonder that they took the romantic name of prairie-schooner, for many of them had jury-rigged masts and a spread of canvas to assist the labouring teams of horses, mules and bullocks when an east wind blew in their favour!

By no means all the gold seekers travelled in such a style. A newspaper of the day carried this moving account by a contributor who had made the journey and returned to tell his tale:

One came hourly upon hand-carts and foot-men slowly journeying over the undulations of the plains. Not a few of them had started out with only such clothing as they wore on their backs, and small bags containing a few pounds of corn meal and meat. We met two individuals, one fifty and the other sixty-two years old, who had left with just 20 lbs. of corn and only 1.68 dollars in money. There were innumerable poor hand-cart and foot-men hungry, in rags, shoeless, with sore and swollen feet and without shelter from the rains and chilling winds. Not a few had to meet death in its most awful form, starvation; and, what is worse, were driven by the maddening pangs of hunger to acts of *cannibalism*, such as living on human flesh, even on brothers' bodies. The trails were lined with cooking-stoves, clothing and even mining tools, thrown away to lighten loads; and with the rotting carcasses of horses that had perished on the way. Also with many *fresh* graves. Upon a secluded island in the Platte were the bloody remains of a little girl with a broken skull. It is difficult to surmise the motive of the murder of the poor child.

There were other hazards, and in the comparatively few genuine guide-books, drawn up by men who had in fact made the journey, even found some gold, and returned to tell the tale, information was given which must have been deeply pondered by prospectors who had yet to amass the necessary capital to venture forth. The Indians, in particular, were an unknown quantity and it was as well that due warning and advice should be offered:

The tribes likely to be met on this route are the Pawnees, the Sioux, the Cheyennes and the Arraphoes. The *less* said to Indians, the *better*. If they are met, and manifest a friendly spirit, extend to them the usual salutation and *pass on*, manifesting *no fear*, and as little *emotion* as possible. If you make trade with an Indian and he is not satisfied, trade back *without hesitation*. The principal danger of collision arises from meeting a War Party. The *braves* are usually on horseback, and in approaching they frequently ride as though about to make a *charge*, when in reality they are only excited by curiosity. If they demand presents, they will usually leave after a gift of flour or tobacco. Should this fail, and there is danger of collision, the best weapon that can be used is an *ox-goad*, or *whip*. Let some stout man seize his whip and *thrash* away at them, and they will run much sooner and faster than if a dozen had been killed.

The advice offered carries the ring of experience; all the same, one would have supposed that in a region like Colorado and among such a rabble of men as drifted there in search of gold, the gunshot would come first and the ox-goad or whip a poor second! However, the compiler of another guide-book had advice to offer that was more subtle:

Indians sometimes bear papers from which you will learn that "the Bearer is a Chief, intelligent and brave, and earnestly desires a little flour, sugar and coffee". The best thing, then, is to treat them well *invariably*. If they come in bands of three or four, feed them; if in bands of hundreds, feed their Chiefs. But watch them *constantly*, or they will steal everything you have. Trade with them freely if you need their moccasins, robes or belts; but keep your arms in good order and always ready for use. Finally: Be *kind*, and yet always *cautious*!

Guide-books were advertised as containing "Maps compiled from surveys and notes taken *on the grounds* by a practical engineer, together with tables showing camping-places and also distances between same on various routes. Price One Dollar." And it is easy to visualize the impact of such an advertisement on the gullible reader: Here, he would exclaim, is all I need to become wealthy. One Dollar, and the whole of Pike's Peak is mine!

On the other hand, there were guide-books in which emphasis was laid on the purely descriptive. Internal evidence suggests that these were the work of men who had allowed their imaginations to supply what their experience had withheld:

> We started out, taking with us a few days' provisions, to prospect among the headwaters of the River Platte. For eleven days we travelled over craggy, stupendous rocks and mountains. Our clothing, which was good when we set out, was torn from off our backs and our skin and flesh mangled by the craggy surface of the rocks. We reached many places where it seemed impossible for anything save the feathered tribe to survive. Wild animals of almost every species inhabit these mountains. Our provisions being eventually exhausted, we were compelled to subsist on game. We killed black, brown and grizzly bears, elk and mountain sheep. One ram was shot whose weight could not have been less than 500 pounds. Panthers and Pumas often came in sight. In order to get some fresh meat for breakfast one morning, we went out in pursuit of game and shot a large deer on the edge of a very dense thicket. No sooner had it fallen, however, than a *lion* seized upon it and carried it to his jungle lair without difficulty....

The adventurous-minded youth, reading such a description of the hazards to be met with *en route* to Colorado, may have had his imagination fired as much as his covetousness had been excited by the advertisements; more sober individuals, however, may have raised an eyebrow at the remarkable variety of fauna allegedly to be

encountered in a region where a thicket becomes a jungle within
two lines, and the panther, puma, grizzly and lion compete for
living-space with the deer and mountain sheep!

The newspapers for a while throve on the advertisements of the
bogus prospectors, the stay-at-home "experts" and the swarming
speculators. But to read their columns as the months went by is to
find a new note appearing in them: the note of disillusionment. The
editors who retained a little integrity, who could afford not to
pander to the vested interests, began to accept letters for publication
such as this from a returned gold seeker:

> Sir, permit me, through the medium of your excellent news-
> paper, to say a few things concerning the Pike's Peak diggings.
> I have just returned, and am surprised to learn the excitement
> which exists with reference to them—an excitement *for which
> there is no cause*, believe me! Unprincipled men, who have some
> ulterior design or motive in view, have been feeding the public
> mind with marvellous tales of the auriferous richness of the region.
> Since my return, I have frequently been asked: "What have you
> done this season, out there?" My answer has always had to be
> "NOTHING!" Our party numbered 103 men. We did as much
> prospecting as was necessary, but our season's labour yielded us
> 18 DOLLARS—and this not individually but *altogether*. On our
> return, we met many going out to spend the winter there. Many
> of them, I fear, will perish. I would warn those who have not yet
> started, to defer setting out before Spring. They can do *nothing*
> (even if there *were* gold) this Winter. I would advise any who
> can make from 50 cents to a dollar a day *at home* to stay at home.
> They will not make even so much, out there.

It was admirable advice—which was taken by all too few.
Advice, argued the know-alls who had yet to learn the hard way,
given by the gutless who had not had the courage and determination
to push farther into the hills and win the gold which, assuredly,
was there to be won. The promoters of Pike's Peak, the speculators, the get-rich-quick shopkeepers and real-estate men, the
suppliers of tools and equipment, the horse dealers, blacksmiths
and wheelwrights called in to repair and refurnish tormented
prairie-schooners: these men did well; at the expense very literally
of scores of thousands of dupes blinded by the shadowy promise of
gold.

FOUR

The Trail of '98

"Wild and wide are my borders,
Stern as Death is my sway;
From my ruthless throne I have ruled alone
For a million years and a day;
Hugging my mighty Treasure,
Waiting for Man to come. . . ."
Robert W. Service.

OF all gold rushes, the one which has caught and fired the imagination most completely is the Yukon, or Klondike, gold rush— the almost legendary "Trail of '98". Almost legendary, not because it is remote in time: it was a half-century later than California, forty years later than Colorado, and there are men alive today who took part in it as youngsters and have survived to tell the tale; but because of the conditions under which it took place.

Any memories of it must be bitter: bitter, and cold. It is the appalling cold, the animal-like malevolence of nature at her most cruel, the diabolical harshness of the Yukon in the grip of winter, that predominates over all else.

Winter begins early in that latitude—between 60° and 65° North. By mid-October the tributaries of the Klondike and Yukon Rivers are frozen over; when the temperature has dropped to 15° below, mush-ice appears on the rivers themselves; soon they are covered with a solid sheet of black ice—smooth where movement had been free, craggy where a pile-up had taken place as the frost increased its grip. The whole landscape takes on a nightmarish quality— almost like the imagined moon-scape. Temperatures swiftly drop to 30° below, to 40° below; and there are lower figures before the winter is out. It was into such a bleak, forbidding, desolate territory that men in their thousands followed the winter trail of 1898.

At such temperatures all water had to be sought at the bottom of holes hacked through several feet of ice. The mercury in their thermometers froze and men could only guess at the true temperature: a false estimate, and they could die as a candle flame dies. A few men possessed alcohol thermometers, which would record after mercury had frozen. Some discovered that a popular liniment known as "St. Jacob's Oil" would remain fluid at 75° below: and there were long, dark days and nights when the temperature never rose above this.

It is said that a miner who had heated a little water to do some gold panning saw it freeze in mid-air as it passed from kettle to pan; it cracked in fragments as it fell to the ground! A man's breath froze in the air if he was more than a foot or two from the stove, forming icicles so that he had to cut off his beard before he could rise from his sleeping-bag. If he touched any metal with his bare hand the skin and flesh stuck to it and had to be cut away. Axes had to be kept beneath the stove, otherwise they splintered on impact with the fuel they were intended to cut.

Frostbite was a commonplace, but there were no doctors at hand. If a man was alone, gangrene set in and he died; if he had companions, one of them would heat an axe red hot and, with no more anaesthetic than at best a shot of whisky, amputate hand or arm or leg. When a man died, he was laid out on the ground or the hut roof, for it was impossible to dig a grave in that iron soil.

Scurvy was another commonplace: the traditional diet of great quantities of beans boiled in advance and reheated, mealtime by mealtime, in pans of bacon fat, together with coarse pancakes, quickly ruined the physiques of most prospectors: their gums swelled, their teeth fell out, their limbs and joints were racked with excruciating pain. A point came when a man could not work any more: that was the end, for apathy swiftly overwhelmed him and he would lie down with no further will to live.

Contemporary records mention the finding of hideously bloated corpses in remote creeks where isolated workers had succumbed to the bitterness of their conditions and rotted when the pale Yukon spring replaced the winter; they mention, too, an astonishing case of the will-to-live. A man was found in a stoveless hut, gangrenous from toes to waist, paralysed, but still alive though he had lain there four weeks. His gums were so swollen that they protruded beyond his lips. He had kept himself alive by scraping ice off the hut wall, melting it against his body and mixing flour and sugar with it in a tin so that he could suck the resultant paste with his swollen tongue. He possessed toughness far beyond that of most of his fellow-miners.

The first of these were the so-called "sourdoughs"—nomads without birthplace or nationality that they could remember: Scandinavians, French, Germans, Australians, Americans and Canadians, British and Russians, too, drifted northwards in their wake. But the sourdoughs were inveterate wanderers, tough, self-reliant, enterprising: they derived their name from the one item of equipment common to them all: a can of sour dough on which they throve, washing it down with spruce needle tea. They had worked their way leisurely up the Pacific seaboard of America, over the Canadian border, making for the Yukon and Alaska. And they chanced to find gold there. Fur traders brought the news south by way of Seattle: and thus was sparked-off the trail of '98.

The newspapermen, alert for anything that spelt news in capital letters, interviewed the traders, the captains of the coasting vessels on which they had travelled south—and banner headlines startled the newspaper readers: "Gold . . . Gold . . . Gold! Stacks of Yellow Metal!" "Traders Worth 100,000 Dollars!" "Gold in Seattle Today is Weighed by the 100 lbs.!" "Klondike Treasure: A Ton of Gold!" "Inexhaustible Riches in Northern Eldorado!" "Nuggets From Alaska!"

Rumour vied with rumour. There was gold in lumps the size of guinea-fowls' eggs; as large as potatoes; the size of coconuts! A gold-digger had walked into a newspaper office, slapped down his moose-skin "poke", the traditional wallet of the day, and a solid lump of gold had bounced out of it that was worth, by current prices, 6,000 dollars. "And there are plenty more where that one came from!" he had added. It was California plus Colorado "with knobs on"—and the knobs, allegedly, were purest gold in nuggets of ever-increasing size.

The excitement ran like wildfire through the towns on the Pacific seaboard—and well inland, too. Those who could afford to do so (and many who could not) obtained passages on the coastal vessels heading northwards to St. Michael, planning to change to smaller vessels and work their way up the Yukon River through Alaska and so to the River Klondike and the newly-discovered gold-fields. It was, they understood, the most rapid, and the safest route. For the vast majority, however, a shorter sea passage as far as the labyrinth of creeks, small islets, reefs and rapids of the Alexander Archipelago was all that was possible. They must then make for Wrangell, Juneau or Skagway, some hundreds of miles inland, and then begin the really formidable stage of their long journey north: the final six hundred miles of the trail which included the terrible Chilkoot, or "Poor Man's", Pass.

This was a deadly means of approach; literally deadly. There are few parallels to it in history, outside perhaps Napoleon's great retreat from Moscow through the snows of Russia, which was

echoed a century and more later by the terrible retreat of the
German army from Stalingrad.

The Chilkoot Pass begins deceptively, following the course of the
River Dyea. But suddenly it shoots upwards through a rocky canyon
devoid of trees or any sign of life, aiming for the tongue of the
Chilkoot Glacier which points menacingly downwards, many
thousands of feet higher up. The average gradient on much of the
climb is something like one in three, and for a good part of its length
the track is more like a flight of steep, craggy steps than a pathway:
a gigantic frozen staircase hemmed in between boulders as big as
houses.

Up this, the gold seekers of '98 had to struggle, climbing
laboriously a step or two at a time, dragging reluctant horses and
mules—even pack-dogs; hauling on makeshift sledges; humping
their enormous loads on their backs when their animals proved
unable to negotiate the so-called track any further. Soon the lower
stages of the Chilkoot were strewn with the frozen corpses of the
pack animals which had literally been able to go no further and had
had, therefore, simply to be abandoned beside the track. Late-
comers, who followed when the thaw had set in, reported afterwards
that there were corpses of animals and men by the score, that the
upward trail "stank like an abattoir".

Gradually the hundreds, the thousands of prospectors strung out
more and more thinly on the Chilkoot. Groups of them tried
organizing shuttle-services, humping a portion of their joint load
so far up the track and then returning for more, till the load was
complete. A diary kept by one of these has the entry: "A week
moving 4,500 lbs. 5 miles. Temperature 17° below, but clear."
Another entry is even more revealing of the mood of the gold seekers,
the undercurrent of bitterness, frustration, jealousy, fear: "Nobody
speaking on the trail. We move forward like dead men. Not even a
howl out of the dogs. The dogs are the only decent members of this
party. R. pulled his knife on me yesterday. May be I deserved it.
This would be a hell of a place to be left. Would H. bury me, I
wonder?"

There is plenty of evidence that men quarrelled violently at the
slightest provocation; even without provocation—other than the
perpetual, inescapable challenge of the icy Chilkoot itself, which
assumed, for all of them, the characteristics of a deadly, an implacable foe. However amicably and hopefully men had set out
together, the seed of discontent soon appeared: a partner was not
doing his fair share of hauling; he was making secret inroads on the

precious store of food; he was malingering, slowing the others down. Knives were quick in action. The icy wind flayed the skin; no amount of bacon fat smeared over the face—the standard poor man's panacea—proved a lasting protection; the eyes swelled; shoulders were rubbed raw by the huge loads that had to be continually shrugged on and off as the carriers negotiated the man-high frozen steps; and hardly a man of them but suffered the demoralizing effects of dysentery.

A man who stopped to rest found that the sweat froze to his skin beneath his clothes. If he tried to free his clothes, his skin tore off in strips. He was overtaken by others coming up behind, and kicked ruthlessly to one side as they tried to keep together, so that he was separated from the rest of his party. The chances of overtaking them were small. He might try a burst of speed—only to miss his step and plunge into some crevasse hidden by a thin crust of hard snow. The rest of his party, ahead of him, would not know what had happened; those behind him, who watched, had troubles enough of their own without bothering over a stranger: the Chilkoot was no haunt of Good Samaritans.

Beyond the summit of the Chilkoot Pass, those who made it found, of course, that the going was now downhill, and therefore that much the easier. They descended at length to the swampy ground through which shallow tributaries of the Yukon River flowed; and now there was a fresh hazard, the so-called Yukon Mosquito. There is hardly a Klondiker's diary that does not contain references to this devilish creature. Some of the men positively stated that they would endure the climb to the summit of Chilkoot Pass twice over, rather than face this new menace. In one of them there is this passage:

The mosquitoes were like smoke in the air and were distinguished by the reckless daring of their attack. Thousands might be killed, yet the survivors carried on the war. A blanket offered them no impediment; buckskin alone defied them. At meal times, forced to remove our nets, we sat until nearly stifled in the smoke, and, emerging for a breath of air, received no mercy. My companions' hands were nearly raw, and I can well conceive that a man without a net in one of these marshes would soon die from nervous exhaustion. The mosquitoes are so thick at times that I could not take accurate aim with my rifle to shoot game for my party. . . .

Many a man who had not left with the advance party and who

may have found the Chilkoot, in spring, less of an ordeal than he had
supposed from the reports of it that had reached him before he set
out, must have wished he had crossed those swamps before the
temperature rose near enough to freezing from its unbelievable
depths to release the Yukon Mosquito. But all in all, the bitterest
enemy was the ice, the Arctic winds that funnelled down from the
glacier at the summit of the Chilkoot, the blizzards of snow that
sprang up without warning and descended the pass like a myriad
bayonet-armed invisible soldiers. Robert W. Service caught the very
spirit, the breath, of the Chilkoot in mid-winter when he wrote:

> "One by one I betrayed them unto my manifold dooms;
> Drowned them like rats in my rivers, starved them like curs
>   on my plains;
> Rotted the flesh that was left them, poisoned the blood in their
>   veins;
> Burst with my winter upon them, searing forever their sight;
> Lashed them with fungus-white faces, whimpering wild in the
>   night;
> Staggering blind thro' the storm-whirl, stumbling mad in
>   the snow;
> Frozen stiff in the pack-ice, brittle and bent like a bow;
> Featureless, formless, forsaken, scented by wolves in their
>   flight,
> Left for the wind to make music thro' ribs that are glittering
>   white;
> Gnawing the black crust of failure, searching the pit of
>   despair. . . ."

Their goal throughout this interminable journey was Dawson
City, at the confluence of the Yukon and Klondike Rivers. When
the gold rush began, it was a collection of small timber hutments
containing some four hundred inhabitants; within a few months
its population rose to 5,000; and in the next few months that figure
rose to 30,000—and was to keep on rising as wave after wave of
gold seekers poured into the district. Improvised huts, home-made
tents, roofed-over boats on the rivers: these were the homes of the
Klondikers in the early stages; nor is it surprising that the largest
of these groups of makeshift habitations came to be known as
"Louse Town".

Gradually, however, some sort of attempt was made to create
law and order out of the surrounding chaos. Timber-framed

"The Alchemist" by Breughel

Main Street, Dawson City, during the Klondike gold rush

Prospectors panning for gold, California

buildings were erected; streets were hammered out and an attempt made to pave them if only with rough stone and rubble; water was piped from the nearest river to the largest of these new congeries of habitations, and the grandiose name, Klondike City, was tacked on to it. It was the centre of an area in which some thousands of claims were staked out, to be worked by tens of thousands of gold diggers. The two "cities"—and the term was a misnomer if ever there was one—expanded opposite one another, vying with one another in the amenities they could offer.

The amenities were few, but basic: a miner, when he came in from working his claim, wanted drink, and a woman. He also wanted to off-load his gold dust. Partly so that he need not have to keep watch every moment of the day and night lest someone filched it from him; and partly so that he had in exchange for it the necessary dollars to buy the two basic pleasures he had come to town for. Every other building carried the sign: Gold Dust Bought, or its equivalent. And the intervening buildings catered for his other needs. Dawson City and Klondike City were not, by moral or any other standards, healthy spots in 1898 and the years immediately following.

It is not surprising that only a handful of gold seekers brought their womenfolk with them. But those who made early lucky strikes and were able to pay the passage-money demanded on vessels trading between San Francisco and St. Michael, Alaska, did in some cases fetch them from home to keep house for them. Or, if they had no womenfolk of their own, they put advertisements in newspapers. For example: "Any woman, innocent or full of guile, can become a bride without delay. She will have a wedding present of a thousand dollars from her groom within *thirty* minutes after she arrives in Dawson City."

Dawson City, when its population had swollen to 5,000, still had only a hundred women living there: a woman had a choice of fifty men; it was a sellers' market with a vengeance! A speculator in New England tried to raise the funds to ship 4,000 unmarried women there, but his project fell through! However, rumour soon reached the unmarried women in all parts of the United States that there was a shortage of that essential commodity in the Yukon. It was not long before newspapers began to carry advertisements such as this one that appeared in the town of Marysville:

A HUSBAND WANTED—by a Lady who can wash, cook, scour, sew, milk, spin, weave, hoe (can't plow), cut wood, make fires, feed the pigs, raise chickens, *rock the cradle* (but gold-rocker, I thank you, Sir!), saw a plank, drive a nail, etc. These are a few of her solid accomplishments. Now for the Ornamental ones. She can read Murray's *Geography* and find 6 States on the Atlas. Can read—and you can see that she can write! Could paint roses, butterflies, etc., but will paint houses, whitewash fences etc. Could once dance. Can ride a horse, donkey or ox. I hear you ask: Can she *scold*? No, she can't! As for her terms: her age is none of your business. She is neither handsome nor a fright; yet an *old* man need not apply, nor any without education. Gold? There must be 20,000 dollars settled on her before she will bind herself to perform all the above. Address your reply to Dorothy Scraggs, P.O., Marysville, giving your *real* name.

She deserved an answer, and one likes to think that the right man saw that advertisement, sent up from his home town and read in the flickering light of his shack on some such claim as Ophir, Eureka, Hunker, Quartz, Sulphur Creek, Bear, All Gold or Sixty-Mile, answered it, and got this most enterprising and obviously accomplished helpmeet!

One Klondiker's diary records the fact that unmarried girls were so anxious to get to Dawson City and find themselves husbands with such prospects that they would go to any lengths to organize passages for themselves. He himself was approached by a "hostess" in a dance-hall of his home town, to which he had returned for a brief visit, and asked when he would be going back to the Yukon. He told her that he was leaving almost immediately. She promptly begged to be permitted to accompany him. She would, she said, give him her life's savings of a thousand dollars to purchase the necessary travelling equipment on her behalf. She would cook, sew, darn and wash for him *en route*, and sleep with him as often as he wished. Furthermore, when they reached Dawson City and she had established herself and started making money in the only way she knew, she would undertake to hand over a percentage of her earnings until such time as she married. As an added inducement, she offered to go into harness with his huskies, if necessary, provided he undertook "to go easy on the whip".

A New York girl was more subtle. The editor of the newspaper called *Dawson City Nugget* received a letter saying: "Kindly place this photograph in a prominent place in your window. The first man who calls to ask about it, tell him he is to give you the money for this advertisement before you give him my address." The advertisement was enclosed. It contained what today would be called her "vital statistics". She was twenty years old. She was honest (or naïve) enough to state explicitly that she wanted a rich husband. Her photograph caused a queue of applicants to line up within half an hour of its being placed in the window, and every man-jack of the applicants offered gold dust in payment! The New York girl received her replies, made her choice and (one hopes, somewhat dubiously) lived happily with him ever afterwards.

But Dawson City was not a promising centre for happy domestic life: it was too unnatural. The majority of the ever-growing population of women had not gone there with the idea of marriage: they were gold diggers in the secondary sense. And the market remained a sellers' market. Nor did a girl need good looks: stamina, a cold, calculating eye and utter ruthlessness in competition were her essential characteristics. It was very rare for one of them to need more than a week or two to recoup her expenditure on the northward journey from her home town.

The records of Dawson City in its heyday abound with stories of foolish men who sacrificed weeks and months of arduous work in isolated "benches", as the prevailing type of gold site was called, by handing over a "poke" of gold dust for the doubtful pleasures of a night or two with a Dawson City girl. Just now and then, however, the tables are nicely turned; as, for instance, in the pleasant tale of a Klondiker nicknamed "Dog-Tooth Harry".

Dog-Tooth Harry was ugly even by Klondikers' standards. A girl had to be very drunk indeed before she would look a second time in his direction. Which was a pity, because in fact Harry was a serious-minded Klondiker; he wanted just one thing: to get married. He had spent half a lifetime being rebuffed by every eligible girl he approached with this end in view. And one day he fell head over heels in love with one of the Dawson City dance-hall girls. She was handsomer than most, and her price was high; so high that she scared away more men than she hooked. Your "poke" had to be well filled indeed, if she was to show any interest in you.

Dog-Tooth Harry proposed marriage to her, and she laughed. Tirelessly, he pursued her, offering her a home and comfort and security; a change from her present life. And as tirelessly, she rejected him, seeking every opportunity to hold him up to ridicule. One day, however, she announced that she was worth her weight in gold; and would sell herself for not an ounce less.

Dog-Tooth Harry took up the challenge. Quick as a flash, he snatched her off the dance-hall floor and carried her bodily, at a

brisk trot, to the nearest booth with the sign "Gold Dust Bought".
Dropping her on to one pan, he slung weights into the other, and
found she tipped the scales at just 142 lbs. On current rates that
represented 24,424 dollars.

Still spitting and screaming her indignation, he left her to wriggle
off the scales, and ran back to his base. There he collected from its
secret hiding-place all the gold dust he could lay his hands on.
Returning to the booth, he had 142 lbs. of it weighed out, and
exchanged it for 24,424 dollars in bills. And with these, he returned
to the dance-hall and the girl.

As he had expected, she now very swiftly changed her tune:
24,424 dollars was quite a sum! Here was a man after her own heart.
He had accepted her at her own valuation, and had returned with
her weight in cash. She ceased to spit and snarl and deride. She
strenuously asserted that she had been joking all along. She threw
her arms round Dog-Tooth Harry's neck and offered her practised
lips for a kiss. He was, she assured him for all to hear, the hand-
somest man in all Dawson City.

Dog-Tooth Harry disengaged her clutching hands from behind
the collar of his mackinaw. Looking her full in the eye, he thrust the
thick wad of bills back into an inner pocket. And then, with force
and great accuracy, he spat contemptuously on to the ground
between her feet, and walked out.

Dog-Tooth Harry's "claim" was only one of some ten thousand
claims, varying enormously in output, in the bleak territory
surrounding Dawson City. Some men struck it rich almost at once,
sold out, and returned to their home towns. A claim would change
hands at about 5,000 dollars if it was an as yet "unproved" claim;
if it had already yielded good "pay dirt" it would change hands
for ten times that amount, the new owner being prepared to dig
deeper, and longer, than his predecessor. Others dug for weeks,
always believing their luck would turn; then lost heart and packed
up, their savings as well as their patience exhausted. The "pay-
streak" usually lay immediately over bedrock; the layer of muck
above it varied in depth, and in hardness. Water to wash the dirt
and reveal the dust was essential; but not always at hand.

Summer digging was strenuous enough; winter digging was
purgatory. It involved thawing out patches of ground by lighting
and tending fires over them till the surface was at least loose enough
for a pick point to enter it, instead of splintering on impact as so
many did. Yukon soil in winter was frozen often to a depth of six
or eight feet. In spite of such difficulty there were Klondikers who

dug with passionate fervour for weeks on end, their eyes reaching out to the promise of the hidden gold. Charlie Anderson was one of these implacable diggers. At the bottom of his first hole he panned 130,000 dollars-worth of gold dust. He left the Yukon to find himself a woman, returned with her to take another 100,000 dollars-worth out of the same hole, and then decided that the Klondike owed him nothing more, and returned to San Francisco to enjoy his affluence. But he was a comparative rarity: Dawson City saw 10,000 Klondikers broke to the wide within the first half-year of the gold rush.

By then the town itself had swelled to 30,000 and more. It was just beginning to regard itself as secure when it was almost entirely destroyed by fire. It was rebuilt; and, in 1899, when the late-April temperature stood at 45° below, it was burnt out for the second time; and it was for the second time rebuilt: there was money in the town, and there were resources in man-power and material which it had not possessed a year or so before.

But its heyday was past. The spate of Klondike-bound gold seekers dwindled; the swarm of men already there thinned out, the "benches" worked to vanishing-point. Some of the miners headed north-by-west, over the Yukon frontier into Alaska, to try their luck elsewhere; some, the lucky minority, departed, satisfied—so far as it can be said that any man is ever satisfied with the gold he has acquired, by fair means or foul—with their winnings; or, alternatively, so reduced in strength and health by the incessant hostility of the climate and the terrain that they could face it no more. By the turn of the century the gold diggers were leaving Dawson City in their thousands: as fast as they had entered it only a couple of years before. Its swift descent into a "ghost town" had begun; and a ghost town it duly became, and remained. In its brief span of life it had seen perhaps more examples of lust for gold and of the effect of this lust on men and on women, too, than any other single town in the world before or since.

FIVE

Fossickers and Nuggets

"Gold is but Muck."
Ben Jonson.

CALIFORNIA, Colorado and the Klondike produced gold in the form of dust or fine grains: anything more substantial was rare indeed. Australia was different: the setting for the really spectacular gold finds. The first came almost as soon as the first reports of the Californian gold rush seeped through to that vast and virtually unpeopled continent. On the morning of July 17, 1851, the *Sydney Morning Herald* splashed a story beneath banner headlines that electrified all who saw it:

A few days ago, an educated aboriginal in the service of Dr. J. W. Kerr returned home with the intelligence that he had discovered a large mass of gold among a heap of quartz upon the sheep run. Gold being the universal topic, the curiosity of this sable son of the forest was excited, and, provided with a tomahawk, he had explored the country adjacent to his employer's land, and had thus made the discovery. His attention was first called to the lucky spot by observing some glittering yellow substance. He applied his tomahawk and broke off a portion— and at that moment the splendid prize stood revealed to his sight.

His first care was to disclose the discovery to his master, and as might be expected, little time was lost by the worthy doctor. In a very short time the three blocks of quartz, containing the *hundredweight* of gold, were released from the bed where, charged with unknown wealth, they had rested, perhaps for thousands of years, awaiting the hand of civilized man to disturb them.

The largest block was a foot in diameter and weighed 75 lbs. gross. Out of this, 60 lbs. of *pure gold* was taken! Not being able to move it conveniently, Dr. Kerr broke it into small fragments, and herein committed a very grand error, for as a specimen the glittering block would have been invaluable.

The interest in the possibility of finding gold beneath one's feet, prompted by the news from California, received a sudden and tremendous stimulus. If a "sable son of the forest", armed only with a tomahawk, men argued, could have this sort of luck, how much better they themselves would fare if they set methodically to work!

And how right they were at that! In the next few years gold nuggets of almost unbelievable proportions and purity continued to crop up in Australia. Their weight was such that they were given names, became personalities: "Sarah Sands" weighed 1,117 ounces —that is to say, a fraction over 93 lbs.; "Lady Hotham", found soon afterwards, tipped the scales at 1,177 ounces; "Blanche Barkeley" reached the most unladylike weight of 1,743 ounces. And then came the first of the real giants: the "Welcome Nugget", of 2,195 ounces, was immediately valued at £9,325, and the "Welcome Stranger", of 2,284 ounces, at £9,534. What they would be worth by today's gold prices, a century afterwards, beggars imagination!

The story of the discovery of this, the largest nugget ever found, has the beauty of simplicity and surprise: small wonder that it sparked-off a tremendous surge of gold seeking. Two men, John Deason and Richard Oates, were dragging their hand-cart along a rutted track softened by unexpected rain. The off-side wheel sank deeply in, and they had to drag their hand-cart back in an attempt to rush it through. It sank in more deeply still. With an oath, Deason snatched up a spade and began to dig to clear the wheel. The spade hit something solid, jarring his wrist. Oates put his shoulder to the hand-cart, and jerked the wheel loose from the rut. And as he did so, he caught the glint of something yellow beneath the edge of the spade.

The two men, suspecting the truth, though never dreaming of the magnitude of what they were to reveal, dug feverishly. It took their united strength to lift the yellow boulder from the clinging mud, for it weighed 200 lbs. Where the spade had scratched it, the surface gleamed unmistakably golden: there was no doubt as to what they had discovered, now!

Because they were in a popular digging area, inappropriately named Black Head, they feared prying eyes; they therefore reburied the boulder exactly where they had found it, covered their tracks, made a mark on a tree, and went on their way. When darkness fell they returned, recovered their precious boulder and manhandled it to their shack, where they stowed it in the thickness of the wall behind the fireplace, lighting a fire for added security. It was as well that they did so, for a couple of neighbouring diggers dropped in for a drink and a grumble. The four men sat for half the night in front of a small fire which screened, as two only of them guessed, fabulous wealth. They must have been anxious, interminable hours!

They were anxious hours, too, during which they conveyed their find to the nearest assayer's office. There they found that the boulder itself weighed 2,520 ounces; and—more important—that the percentage of pure gold in it was so high that it scaled over 2,280 ounces. They pocketed close on £10,000 for that chance find that was due simply to a ditched hand-cart wheel!

Though there were these spectacular finds, the bulk of Australia's gold, like that of California, was found the hard way. The Australian gold seeker was a fossicker—a footloose individual who wandered interminably, like the Klondike sourdough, with one eye on the ground beneath his feet and the other on the horizon: his squint was frequently a profitable element in his roving life.

Some of them became bywords even in their own lifetimes. There was an immigrant from Scotland, named Henderson, who sat down on a bank and began cutting hunks of bread and cheese for his midday meal. He stuck his knife blade into the bank, heard it click on something hard, pulled it out with a practised motion of the wrist and found a nugget not two inches below the surface that proved to weigh 46 ounces. Another fossicker, Pete Brenan, rummaging in a deserted working, came across a nugget that weighed 366 ounces; he was near enough to a bank to trade it in that same afternoon, and he walked out £1,115 richer than he had been that morning! Two fossickers who worked as partners were packing up their gear after panning £700-worth of gold dust when one of them stubbed his toe against a nugget that proved to weigh 157 ounces—a nice bonus to their successful panning!

Their haphazard way of life seems to have been attended by extraordinary vagaries of luck. A couple of men might work for days at a likely spot, and pack up in disgust, having found nothing; and the following day a chance fossicker might linger long enough to try his luck—and pick up, as one of them did, a 54-ounce nugget of outstanding purity. He was hungry, and exchanged his find with an opportunist near by for the price of a meal and a drink; and the opportunist promptly had the nugget assayed and sold it for £170! Fossickers remembered, with some bitterness, hearing of a complete amateur undeserving of the proud title, who, equipped with nothing better than a table-knife and a bent spoon, scooped up 16 ounces of gold in less than no time.

Men who threw in their lot together, with the idea that they would augment their chances even if they had to share their profits, had the same unaccountable luck. A party of eight, for instance, sank a shaft in a promising spot and took £13,000-worth of gold from it before deciding they had tapped its last resources. Greedy for the last stiver they might hope for, they persuaded a group of newcomers to the district that they would do well to buy the "good-will" of the site. They offered it, together with their picks and spades, for £70.

After they had left, the newcomers started work. In their first day they won £2,000-worth; on the second and third, a further £8,000-worth; then they, too, sold out. A third party bought the "goodwill"—and cleared a further £37,000 before they finally abandoned it! Such were the turns and twists of fortune in those mid-century years. The gold diggers were perennial optimists. Which is not surprising, since ever and anon there were these spectacular finds to stimulate fresh hope.

New South Wales, and especially Victoria, were the great gold-hunting grounds. The roads running westwards from Sydney, hardly used till then, became suddenly congested with drays, men on horseback, men footslogging, singly or in small, mutually suspicious groups. On the one hand there were the prosperous who sought greater prosperity: convoys of great wagons each carrying four or six or even eight men and a mountain of gear, like the American prairie-schooners. On the other hand there were the old and destitute.

Yet even these sometimes belied their appearance. A newspaper account tells of a pitiable old man wheeling a barrow containing the entire possessions of his wife and family and himself. His small son was harnessed to leather traces; his elderly wife, with a baby in a shawl slung on her back, trudged behind. By contrast with the convoys travelling westwards to the gold diggings, it was a pitiable sight indeed, as the little party tramped the rough road back to Sydney. But the old man wheeled his barrow right in through the doors of the first bank he came to, pulled a couple of tattered blankets off it, and handed over £1,000-worth of gold in dust and small nuggets to the astonished cashier!

Fossickers generally seem to have been less prone to keep diaries than the men who blazed the trail of '98. But one of them, James Bonwick, actually wrote and had published a little book, modestly titled *Notes of a Gold Digger*. There are only forty-odd small pages; but every one of them breathes authenticity. He was a man who had won gold the hard way, and felt he had some advice to offer. He set it down in print in 1852. Like many men who have worked on their own he has acquired a certain philosophy; and there is a quaintness about his style that adds charm to what he has to say:

Gold fields [he wrote] have a most bewitching influence upon fallen humanity. The very name begets a spasmodic affection of the limbs, which want to be off. Man, as a mere lover of beauty, cannot help wishing to look upon the pretty mineral in its virgin home of seclusion, and his acquisitiveness pants to possess the loveliest Darlings ever rocked in a cradle. . . .

He becomes practical, urging the novice not to encumber himself with too much luggage:

By all means, though, provide yourself with good stout clothes and boots, a coat and trousers of *oilskin cloth*, a roll of canvas and a decent jacket for Sundays, when you ought to appear *civilized*. Spare yourself the anxiety of having your own conveyance. Beware in any case of a *jibber*: there are few things in life more *undesirable* than pushing behind a cart at every piece of rising ground or watching it approaching a precipice while impelled by an animal that will persist in going *crabwise* . . . !

Bonwick advises his readers not to place too much reliance on the tales of huge nuggets unearthed here, there and everywhere: they are exaggerated:

I will, however, suppose you are fairly started. You are rather nervous, yet sanguine. Sundry brave stories keep up your spirits. You are told of a fellow, benighted in the bush, who could not sleep by reason of the hardness of the ground. By morning-light he ascertains that he has chanced to throw himself down upon a nest of nuggets! You hear of a bullock driver in want of a goad, who pulled up a wattle—and found hanging at the root a whole family of nuggets like a brotherhood of potatoes—yet he was in too much of a hurry to bother to pick them up! You will be passed by lots of returning diggers. Some are carrying bags of treasure—and some, aches and pains to the hospital! There is some difference between your smooth chin and their rough beards; your prim appearance, and their soiled garb. . . .

Speaking from experience, and realizing that nothing will dissuade the would-be gold digger from setting forth, he offers a revealing picture:

> Once upon the spot, you are ready to go to any newly discovered Gully of Wonders. You strike your claim, mark your boundaries; and then to vigorous exercise of muscle! Soon the topsoil is off. All goes smoothly till your pick comes in contact with something that soon drives it back again, with loss perhaps of its steel point. A harder thrust, and again your tool rebounds. *Never despair!* Blows thick and fast descend, until an entrance is gained and some insignificant pieces are knocked off. You pause to gather breath and strength. "Why, I have got into something, here!" you exclaim. Some neighbouring bearded digger condescendingly remarks that it is only "burnt stuff" and that you must "drive away". . . .

It is not an encouraging picture; nor does Bonwick intend it to be. But he relents, and concedes that the newcomer has at last extracted a small quantity of the precious metal, the "loveliest Darling ever rocked in a cradle". He hurries back to his hut, too excited even to eat: he must light a fire, for the gold dust has yet to be dried, and proved:

> A spade is put on the fire and the contents of your matchbox poured on to it. Soon the moisture disappears. The dust is then carefully blown away, the magnet is passed over it to take up the iron particles, the little gathering is weighed—and the result is known. Guesses are made as to the value. If six buckets fill a tub, and if ten tubs shall have produced you that day 8 *ounces of gold*. . . .!

All that digging and panning for a hypothetical scatter of gold-bearing dust! Still—things can be better. He rummages among his memories, and offers encouragement to the beginner:

> It is true that many who have dug nineteen holes in vain have dropped upon gold in their twentieth. Four men of my acquaintance were weeks without luck, when they fell in with 75 lbs. weight. Another man was four months unlucky and badly in debt when he came suddenly on £500-worth. Two parties worked alongside for three months; the one did not pay its expenses,

the other took 98 lbs. of gold! At the foot of a tree three fellows took out £1,800-worth. I knew a man at Bendigo who washed out 9 lbs. of gold from a *nosebag* of dirt. In Peg Leg Gully, 80 lbs. have been taken from holes but three or four feet deep. It got its name when a man with a wooden leg sank into the mud, and stopped short when his peg leg hit a lump of gold. . . .

Bonwick's stories of lucky strikes for a time come thick and fast. But before he closes his little handbook he reverts to his note of caution. A man, he says, must never expect to find gold the first time he drops his pick or spade. He must work hard if he is to have any success in the gold-fields of Ballarat or Bendigo : "Perseverance," he ends, "will accomplish wonders at the diggings—as elsewhere. You must not be downhearted if not successful at first; you must TRY, TRY, TRY AGAIN. . . ."

It is more than a hundred years since James Bonwick laid down his pen, his little book finished. The great days of nugget discovery are long since past. Nevertheless, there are echoes, even today.

One morning early in 1950, a Mr. Albert Smith spotted in a crack in the pavement of Wedderburn's High Street, not forty miles from Bendigo, a golden glint. He extracted a nugget which was promptly valued at £1,100, and, like Dr. Kerr's find a century before, this sparked-off a minor gold rush. Men left their offices, workshops, counters, benches and, in the time-honoured tradition, staked out claims. All the claims were worked, but one man only had any luck: a Mr. Butterworth, who found in his own backyard a nugget worth £1,300.

This stimulated flagging endeavour, but once again the majority of the citizens of Wedderburn returned, disillusioned, to their occupations. Only Mr. Butterworth persisted. He continued to dig throughout March and April. And his persistence paid off. He dug up a second nugget of identical weight, and netted a further £1,300. And what is more, six inches away from this, he dug up a third nugget, on the same bright afternoon: valued at £2,300, this time! With a nice sense of the appropriate, and in the old tradition of naming these finds, he called this the "Wedderburn Nugget": not as romantic as "Lady Hotham" or "Blanche Barkeley"; but then it was not so impressive in size!

James Bonwick would have approved of this Wedderburn citizen who had so well illustrated the wisdom of the old advice: Try, try, try again!

SIX

Bullion Robbery

"From the red gold keep thy finger!"
Scott.

THE contemporary street hold-up of wages clerks is today's echo
of the old-time hold-ups practised on the stage-coaches in America in
the days of the gold rushes. But there is a fundamental difference:
today's hold-ups are almost invariably accompanied by violence to
the person; the stage-coach hold-ups, on the other hand, seem to
have been gentlemanly affairs in which personal injury was
studiously avoided. Indeed, there is an aura of romance about these
episodes—at least, when considered after a lapse of a century. It
is possible, however, that the victims whose gold dust and other
personal property so dramatically changed hands may have felt
otherwise about them at the time, and maybe for long afterwards.

There were few long-distance stage-coaches that did not include
in their freight a consignment of gold. It may have been a quantity
of bullion; it may have been no more than a few "pokes" of gold
dust bought by some opportunist from the miners on location and
now being transported to a bank or refinery. But whether large or
small, these consignments of gold seem to have had the quality
of magnets: they attracted the roving, clutching hand; the drivers
knew well that their prospects of an uninterrupted run were
relatively slight.

Roads in those days ran for many miles at a stretch through
virtually empty country. Empty, that is, of habitations; but
unhappily for the traveller, very well wooded. There was always
ample cover for the highwayman. One of these, whose activities
were on a scale sufficient to make him a byword among travellers
and drivers alike, was Sidney Jake.

He was obviously a man of imagination, as well as of the courage
necessary for a man who preferred to operate single-handed. His
"beat" was for a time the highway between the gold-mining township of Auburn and Sacramento. One day he held up the stage-coach

and, at pistol-point, marched the driver and passengers a long mile into the thick brushwood that conveniently grew alongside his beat, then possessed himself of their weapons and of the valuables they had on their persons.

He then turned about and raced back through the brushwood to the coach, donned the driver's hat, which had fallen off in his haste to descend, and drove off at a spanking rate. Having reached his destination, he announced himself as a relief driver deputizing for the regular driver who, he said, had been taken ill. He then loaded up with a full complement of passengers and an express box heavy with bullion, and immediately set out on his return journey with new horses.

When he was well away from his starting-point, in a stretch of desolate country, he brought his coach to a standstill, announcing that it had a hot axle. He ordered his passengers to alight, robbed them one by one of their personal valuables, emptied the contents of the express box into a pair of specially devised capacious saddle-bags and shot all the horses save one, over which he threw his saddlebags. He then leapt on to its back and in a matter of seconds had vanished among the trees.

There were no telegraph lines along those makeshift roads, and little traffic to carry news from point to point. A hold-up such as the double-barrelled one so nimbly engineered by Sidney Jake might remain unreported for a very long time. Anyone who travelled with valuables knew the risks he was running. How his heart must have sunk when the outskirts of the town faded behind him and his conveyance entered the notorious stretches of country with trees or brushwood stretching to the horizon on each side of his road. And how much deeper it must have sunk when his alert ear caught the clip-clop of a swift horse's hoofs closing in on him!

The rewards of such hold-ups were often very great. Some years after the beginning of the Californian gold rush a prosperous jeweller and dealer in gold left his home town with the idea of cashing-in on the swiftly increasing prosperity of San Francisco, into which wealth was pouring in spate. A few miles east of Lake Salt a single horseman with a pistol in each hand brought the coach to a standstill. A harsh voice bade him empty his pockets, and he had no option but to obey. Some instinct, as sharp as that of the Customs Officers, led the horseman to look a little deeper into the contents of an unassuming parcel which the unhappy dealer was endeavouring to conceal behind him. It contained his entire stock of gold and jewellery—a matter of some 30,000 dollars-worth. In a matter of a minute or less, it had vanished with the horseman into the dusk of a Californian evening.

As the first heady wine of the Californian gold rush went flat, many gold seekers accepted the hard truth that there was no guarantee of success with pan and rocker. There was, however, the more astute among them quickly recognized, a better and easier way of making money: this was to let others do the digging and crushing and panning, and then relieve them of their hard-earned gold when it was on its way to the banks and refineries. More and more disillusioned miners sold their claims, invested in a good horse, and took to the open road—and particularly the country that bordered it.

One such was Black Bart, a man whose notoriety soon rivalled that of Sidney Jake himself. His operations were characterized by a meticulous attention to detail. He had a run longer than most of his contemporaries, and more profitable, too, than most: obviously attention to detail paid handsome dividends. In fact, it would almost seem that he enjoyed strategy for its own sake. As the following classic example well illustrates.

He took a room one day at a hotel which he knew to be a regular staging-point for coaches on a gold run. He made a point of engaging the manager, hotel porter and other members of the staff in conversation so that he established himself properly with them from the start. When dusk began to fall, he mentioned that he was tired and proposed to go early to bed. He took his candle, said goodnight, and went upstairs. Once in his room, the first thing he did was to cut an inch or so off the *bottom* of his candle, which was a new one, and then replace it in its holder.

Later, he heard the stage-coach arrive; heard the passengers dining; heard the horses being changed in readiness for the scheduled departure, the time of which he had been careful to ascertain in advance. He slipped away unseen from his bedroom, crossed a field behind the hotel and jumped into a row-boat moored to a stake on the bank of a stream, crossed over, skilfully caught and mounted a horse grazing in a field, and set off in the direction of the ford some miles distant by which he knew the coach would have to pass.

It was a nicely calculated spot for a hold-up, for the stream bed was soft and the banks steepish. He waited as the coach drew near, swinging round the bend and slowing to negotiate the ford. Its wheels dug deep into the mud, the horses plunged and reared, the driver lashed at them in vain—for Black Bart as well as the opposite bank confronted them! The panic-stricken passengers unloaded their valuables, cursing the driver for being such a fool as to land them in such a predicament; and the solitary horseman galloped off into the darkness with the sound of their curses in his ears.

Long before the stage-coach had been extricated from the mud, reversed, and driven back to the hotel, Black Bart was back in his room, his profitable haul stowed among his baggage. He had the good sense to realize that if he were to show no interest in the tumult raised by the returned, despoiled travellers it might look suspicious. He therefore picked up his candle and descended the stairs, mildly inquiring as to the cause of the disturbance. The driver, almost beside himself with rage and frustration, unwisely shouted: "That's the man who held up my coach! I know his beard."

Black Bart smiled indulgently at this irrational outburst and raised an inquiring eye at the manager with whom, not so many hours before, he had been chatting, and at the hotel porter, from whom he had received his new candle.

"Nonsense," said the manager, stoutly. "I was talking with this gentleman myself only an hour ago, and saw him go upstairs to bed with his candle."

Black Bart yawned, and pointed to his candle, the length of which clearly showed how long it had been burning. The stump he had providently cut off its base he had been careful to throw into the stream. He did not bother to refute what the angry driver had said: it was beneath the dignity of a respectable hotel guest. He offered his commiserations to the unhappy passengers, expressed the hope that the remainder of their journey would be uneventful, and betook himself to his bedroom once again

For all his attention to detail, his elaborate scheming, however, the day came that saw Black Bart's downfall. He had collected some 5,000 dollars-worth of gold dust in a hold-up and was making his customary neat getaway when a chance pistol shot grazed his arm and caused him to drop the handkerchief he was using to mop his brow after the high-speed exercise of the past few minutes. Alas for him, he did not linger to retrieve it; alas, too, the handkerchief carried a San Francisco laundrymark—one of Black Bart's characteristics was that he prided himself on looking, as well as being "the perfect gentleman".

Through the laundrymark he was identified and in due course run to earth. He was sentenced to a longish term in the dreaded San Quentin Penitentiary. When he emerged, he took the opportunity of publicly stating that he had done for ever with highway robbery:

Miners of the Californian gold rush of 1849 with pan and rocker

Ballarat gold-stake, during the Australian gold rush, about 1855

Discovery of attempt to smuggle gold, concealed in a car aboard the *Queen Elizabeth*, from New York to Paris. (*Left*) Gold bullion uncovered by removal of part of the wing. (*Below*) Gold ingots discovered by the New York Customs' authorities.

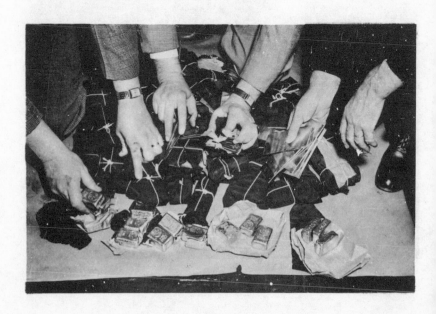

it was a form of activity which, he said, reflection in prison had led him to regard as dishonourable and despicable in the extreme!

Nevertheless, within a few months of his release there were three stage-coach hold-ups which bore certain features in common: each involved a single horseman; each was executed at lightning speed and with great precision; and the express boxes snatched each time, when recovered in due course, were found each to contain a slip of paper on which was written a four-line verse of doggerel advising greater care in future when carrying valuables on the highway. There was only one known operator who had this sense of humour allied to expertise: Black Bart! The Modoc Express Company, the first victim, had little doubt of this; a rival express company, who lost a number of gold bars in the same way a week later, shared the conviction; the Ukiah Stage Coach Company, the third victim, confirmed it. The total value of gold taken by Black Bart in these three close-set hold-ups almost immediately after his release from San Quentin and his public declaration of a change of heart was in the region of 5,000 dollars: it must have helped to boost his morale after the humiliation of being captured through a laundrymark!

Like Robin Hood, Black Bart used to maintain with some emphasis: "I have never stolen from any man who could not afford to lose what I took from him." How he was able to know in advance the pecuniary circumstances of his victims is not clear. It is, however, evident that he made a considerable impression on those with whom he came in contact. "He bears the appearance," one of his victims said, "of a mild, gentlemanly, serious-faced citizen." Doubtless Black Bart capitalized this reputation. The drivers of the Modoc, Ukiah and other stage-coaches, and the passengers they carried, however, may have reflected that no true gentleman or serious-minded citizen would have returned to a life of crime while the echo of his confession of faith was still ringing along the Californian highways.

As railways in California and elsewhere came to succeed the stage-coach, inevitably the hold-up man had to transfer his activities from one to the other: the big freights held greater promise, even if the attendant difficulty and danger were greater in proportion. The latter part of the nineteenth century was a great age for these operations, and even at the beginning of the present century it was estimated that the average haul of gold from the trains was in the region of 150,000 dollars every year.

One of the first big-scale train robberies took place on the Ohio and Mississippi Railway about a hundred miles from Cincinnati,

The train had been some hours on its way and had reached a particularly empty stretch of country when two masked men suddenly appeared on the tender, flourishing four pistols between them, and ordered the engine crew to halt the train, uncouple the passenger coaches from the express car in which bullion was carried, and then haul it along the line until ordered to stop.

After five miles, the pistols were pressed firmly into the backs of the driver and fireman and the brakes applied for the second time. One of the men stayed in the cab, covering the fireman; the other persuaded the driver to open up the express car immediately behind the tender. The messenger inside it was tied up, and his keys taken from him. The safe was rifled and some 12,000 dollars-worth of bullion withdrawn. The two men backed away, still covering the driver and fireman with their pistols, then turned, mounted their horses, which they had tethered in a creek fifty yards away, and sped off cross-country: only the dust cloud in the shimmering air showed the engine crew which way the bullion was now travelling.

Train robberies increased rapidly in number and in scope. Among the most successful gangs operating—for train robbery necessitated a gang rather than the lone highwayman--was the Reno family, Frank, Jesse, Sim and Jack and a co-opted relative. Near Seymour, Indiana, some sixty miles from Cincinnati, they held up a train running on the Indianapolis, Madison and Jefferson line and got clear away with no less than 135,000 dollars-worth of bullion from the express car. Their *modus operandi* was simple, straightforward and very consistently successful. Having obtained information as to the value of the express car freight, they boarded the train unobtrusively at various points, met at an agreed time and place, and proceeded to intimidate the train crew with a spectacular array of weapons. These, in fact, they rarely used; it may be said that they carried on the old tradition of the horseman on the highways, who got his gold by threat rather than violence.

Inevitably, however, the technique of train robbery changed. The railroad companies naturally began to equip their train crews with weapons of defence; and word of this got around among the Renos and their successors. Their gentlemanliness was perhaps only skin deep; certainly the records of train hold-ups after the earliest examples make grim and spectacular reading.

A gang of eight train robbers, for example, tore up a section of the track used by the Chicago, Rock Island and Pacific Railroad Company in Iowa shortly before the fast overland was due. The engine hit the break in the rails at full speed, overturned, ploughed a deep furrow alongside the track and ultimately buried itself in a gully. The leading coaches followed it, and many of the passengers were, like the engine crew, killed, or so badly injured as to be unable to fend for themselves.

Meanwhile, the hold-up men sprang from their places of conceal-ment near at hand, rifled the express car in which the messenger had died, and took many thousands of dollars-worth of bullion from it. Not content with that, they worked their way methodically along the coaches, stripping the dead and dying and injured of their valuables. Any passenger lightly enough injured to make a show of resistance was quickly and mercilessly dealt with: the lust for gold, now, involved deliberate, calculated personal injury and, if necessary, death. The sum of 30,000 dollars was offered for the apprehension of this gang, but the sum was never claimed.

This spectacular and brutal hold-up seems to have been the signal for a long series of train robberies, almost all of them marked by a ruthlessness that had never been associated with hold-ups in the early days. The names of men and gangs such as the Daltons, Sontags, Youngers, James and Evans became bogeys capable of frightening-off prospective train travellers from all but the most essential journeys: it could never be known where they might be going to strike next. The railway companies took the obvious steps: they increased their train crews; they armed them more and more heavily; they had likely sections of their tracks regularly patrolled—a problem indeed when such vast distances were in-volved; they had detectives on the alert for dubious-looking characters boarding their trains at minor halts. But the result was inevitable: the gangs increased in size; they armed themselves more heavily; they penetrated more deeply into terrain that suited their purpose; they became increasingly ruthless in the methods they adopted to halt trains and rifle the express cars. Romance—if it was ever truly present in the stage-coach days—had certainly gone out of highway robbery: the story of American train robberies is an ugly one of blood and murder on railroad tracks successfully organized and prosecuted by gangs who would stop at nothing in their lust for easy, illicit gold.

For obvious reasons there have been few notable gold robberies involving our own railways: gold dust and bullion is not carried about this country as it has been in America. Nor is our countryside as conducive to train hold-ups as the greater, lonelier expanses through which the trans-continental freight trains run. Nevertheless, our railway and bank records do contain one quite outstanding example of a large-scale train robbery of bullion. Outstanding, not because of any dramatic wrecking or massacre such as characterize so many of the bullion robberies on the American railroads, but because of its careful planning, its deft execution, and the value of the bullion stolen. Also, perhaps, for the irony of its postscript.

On the evening of May 15th, 1855, three large chests containing in all nearly two hundredweight of bullion, to a current value of £12,000, were transferred from a carrier's wagon to the guard's van of a train due to leave London Bridge for Folkestone. The chests were securely bound with heavy iron straps; their locks carried the seals of the consignors; the gross weight of each was stamped on lid and underside. They were transferred in the presence of a con- signor's representative and a representative of the South-Eastern Railway, and placed in two safes, each newly fitted with the latest pattern burglar-proof Chubb locking mechanism. The train's guard was instructed not to leave his van for a moment between London Bridge and Folkestone, where the chests would be removed from the safes and transferred to the strong-room of the South-Eastern Railway Company's Channel Packet, which would convey them to Boulogne, where the consignees would be awaiting them.

The train arrived at Folkestone. The two safes were transferred to the Channel Packet, and a few hours later were off-loaded at Boulogne. Before the chests were opened, their weight was checked, against the figure stamped on them and the corresponding figure on the tally-sheet. One chest proved to weigh more, the other two less, than the figures given. They were opened with a set of duplicate keys in the possession of the consignees, and it was found that the bullion in all three of them had been extracted and a quantity of lead shot in canvas bags inserted in its place.

It was, obviously, an "inside" job. The gang, when it was ulti- mately identified, proved to have been a nicely balanced one. It consisted of three railway employees and a co-opted professional thief. James Burgess had been a passenger-train guard for thirteen years; William Pierce was a company's ticket printer; George Tester worked as a clerk in the traffic superintendent's office. The fourth man, Agar, had a criminal record, mainly of larceny, in America and Australia as well as in his native country: it was a nice, cosy set-up all round.

In the traffic superintendent's office, Tester learned that new locks were to be fitted to the company's mobile safes: it was evident that a particularly valuable item of freight was expected. He kept his eyes open, and the day the safes were returned with the new

Chubb locks, together with several sets of keys, for the use of the officials at various transfer-points *en route*, he had little difficulty in borrowing one set, from which Agar quickly made a set for himself.

Chubbs, however, had played a cautious game. Each safe was fitted with two locks; but they differed one from the other and required different keys to open them; moreover, the pairs were not interchangeable. Tester discovered this when he snatched a moment to try out Agar's keys in the locks. In the meantime, he had lost the opportunity to borrow the other keys for Agar to copy. For the moment it was *impasse*.

It was known, however, that there were duplicate sets in the railway company's Folkestone office. Agar therefore arranged for a consignment of valuables—proceeds of another operation—to be dispatched from London Bridge to Folkestone addressed to himself as consignee under an alias. He travelled down to Folkestone a day later to claim his property there. But he insisted on opening the package in the clerk's presence, ostensibly to satisfy himself that there had been no pilfering. It was pure routine for the clerk, of course; but Agar's motive was to discover where the safe keys were kept and what was the simplest means of gaining access to them. When he rejoined his confederates in London he had this information at his fingertips.

The next step involved assistance, and he co-opted Pierce for this. It was necessary to obtain possession, if only for a moment or two, of the keys at Folkestone, to supplement the ones already duplicated in London. The two men entered the office just as the passengers from the newly-arrived Channel Packet were swarming through to the London train. There was the customary confusion. The clerks were run off their feet. Waiting till a moment came when every one of them seemed to be engaged, and with Pierce on hand to engage anyone who momentarily became free, Agar took his chance. He nipped behind the counter, snatched at the key he wanted, squeezed it hard between a fold of prepared wax in the palm of his hand, returned the key to its hook and rejoined his companion. It was as easy as that!

Back in London, Agar completed his set of duplicates. No more could be done until Tester reported from the traffic superintendent's office that the long-looked-for consignment had been received at the station. The news came; on the evening of May 15th the gang closed in.

Burgess was the regular guard on the boat train. If he saw Agar and Pierce arrive on the platform, he ignored them. Indeed, he might not even have recognized them! For they had become, for the occasion, "gentlemen". They were smartly dressed. They had provided themselves with first-class single tickets to Dover—for a reason which will become apparent. A porter followed them lugging a couple of massive leather suitcases. He may have momentarily wondered at their unusual weight, but the tip one of the gentlemen gave him was so substantial that he carried the heavy cases to the guard's van and handed them over to the guard without a murmur. Burgess took them in, possibly smiling grimly to himself at the thought of what they contained. His smile would not be visible through his beard and Dundrearies.

When the whistle blew and the first blasts of steam came from the engine at the far end of the platform, Pierce stepped smartly into his first-class compartment; the other "gentleman" stepped no less smartly—into the still open door of the guard's van. Hardly had the train cleared the station than Agar had whipped out his two pairs of keys and opened the safes. With Burgess's help he withdrew the iron-bound chests containing the £12,000-worth of bullion and broke them open. There were no corridors on trains in 1855, and Burgess knew that there would be no risk of interruption before their first stop, at Redhill.

While Agar scooped out the gold, his confederate, having laid aside his peaked cap, Company's property, replaced it with bags of lead shot from the heavy suitcases so obligingly delivered by the porter. The gold was then packed into the suitcases, wedged with odd pieces of canvas to prevent it from rattling about when they were moved. The lead shot was also packed in with great care (though they were not able to match it with the gold exactly weight for weight), and Agar's practised hand replaced the iron bands on the chests and applied seals that were no bad match for those he had broken. The train slowed down as it ran into Redhill's dimly-lit station. It was an easy enough matter to slip out of the guard's van and rejoin Pierce in his first-class compartment for the remainder of the journey.

At Folkestone the two safes were off-loaded, as anticipated, under the supervision of a Company's representative. Pierce and Agar, however, continued on their way to Dover. At Dover they alighted and secreted themselves until such time as the Ostend–Dover Channel Packet tied up in the harbour. Then, with Ostend–London first-class tickets in their pockets, which they had thoughtfully obtained for themselves well in advance, they mingled with the incoming passengers and boarded the Dover–London train, complete with two massive leather suitcases.

Arrived in London, they walked across to the barrier, carrying their suitcases—rather to the surprise of the porter whose offer they had rebuffed, since in his experience gentlemen as well turned out as they rarely stooped to carrying their own baggage. However, he shrugged his shoulders and looked about for other custom. Agar and Pierce left the station and made for an accommodation address they had arranged well in advance.

They lay low for a while, knowing that a theft of that magnitude would set all the police in London on the watch for suspects. It was the only moment when the three railwaymen may have wished they had not co-opted Agar; but a moment's reflection would have reminded them that without his expertise the bullion robbery could never have succeeded at all. There was no great difficulty about the disposal of the gold, for Agar had a wide connection with the "fences" of London's underworld. The £12,000 was divided in an agreed ratio among the four men, and they thereupon embarked on an elaborate programme of "general post" to avoid any risk of inquiry of a type difficult to answer.

Surprisingly, the hue and cry came to its peak, and died away. The bullion had vanished, and that was that, consignors and consignees appeared to be saying. The police had other tasks on their hands. For two years the four men lived very comfortably and without arousing suspicion. They might have lived even longer in the same way; but unfortunately two of them became involved in a quarrel—over a woman. She ought, according to tradition, to have been pleased that two men should quarrel over her; instead, in a moment of pique, she laid information with the police.

And the upshot? On January 13th, Pierce, Tester and Burgess appeared in the Central Criminal Court to stand their trial for their part in the greatest bullion robbery in English railway history. They received sentences of transportation for a period of fourteen years apiece. Agar, whose trial involved charges over and above this main charge, was sentenced to transportation for life. The considerable proportion of the gold as yet unspent did them little good from that point onwards. Perhaps the woman who brought about their downfall was rewarded out of that residue? It is to be hoped that she got at any rate what she deserved—whatever that was!

It is pure coincidence, of course, that one of the biggest bullion robberies of recent times should have taken place also on May 15th, in the early evening, too: to be exact, at 5.30 p.m. one hundred and two years after the South-Eastern Railway episode. This time, however, it was not a railway job: in accordance with current practice the bullion was being dispatched to its consignee by air.

Overseas visitors, and especially Americans, continue to be surprised at the comparatively casual way in which we in Britain handle gold—treating it very often, in spite of its value, as we treat packages of any kind. The example that follows is a case in point.

At exactly 5 p.m. a B.E.A. van left the Waterloo Air Terminal for London Airport. It carried a driver and a co-driver, the latter acting as security officer because the van was carrying six hundred gold bars, to a value of rather more than £20,000. Half an hour later it was halted by traffic lights at the junction of the Great West Road and Windmill Road, Brentford.

There was a good deal of traffic in both directions and vehicles were travelling pretty close together between each set of lights and the next. The B.E.A. driver was not particularly surprised to feel a slight bump at the rear of his van, for he had braked sharply. Presumably a following vehicle had just touched his rear bumpers. He did, however, glance into his mirror, and what he saw startled him. One rear door was swinging loose on its hinges, and framed in the gap was a man holding in both hands a solid wooden box which he instantly recognized.

"Quick, mate!" he rapped out to his co-driver, and the two of them were out of their seats and racing round to the back of their van in a split second. But that split second was long enough for the man to leap into a van immediately behind; the engine roared and the tyres screamed, and they saw it swerve at high speed into the welter of traffic and vanish from sight.

It was obvious that this, like the South-Eastern Railway bullion theft, was an "inside" job. B.E.A. vans ply between Terminal and Airport all day and every day and a consignment of gold is a rarity. Moreover it was only on the actual morning of the robbery that the Hatton Garden firm dispatching the gold had received instructions from the Swiss consignees to pack it for transit. In the seven or eight at most intervening hours the gold had had to be collected, packed, delivered to the Terminal, checked, weighed and loaded into the van. Someone had worked pretty fast.

It was probably the shortness of the notice that accounted for one basic error of calculation—an error which led to the identification, apprehension and ultimate conviction of the two men concerned. It is customary in cases of robbery to utilize a stolen car: this helps to throw the police off the scent for an hour or two, and the hour or two can make all the difference between success and failure. In this particular case, however, the gold robbers used a van of their own.

The police very quickly found it, and the presence of some large splinters of wood and metal strips on the floor confirmed their suspicions that the van had carried the box of gold and had been the setting for the breaking open of the box and removal of its contents. It was quite easy to identify the owner from the licence, which the thieves in their haste had foolishly omitted to remove. They traced it to a florist's in East London—and were not entirely surprised to find that the florist, whom they knew well by sight, was away from home. Nor were they surprised that no one at home seemed able— or at any rate willing—to say where the absent florist might have betaken himself.

One of the police recalled that the florist was often to be seen with a street trader in the same line of quite legitimate business. They made inquiries, located the street trader's address—and once again were not in the least surprised to find that he too had left home and none of his neighbours seemed to know either when or where he might perhaps be found.

Throughout the following weeks the police went unobtrusively about their work, following up possible clues, and in due course they ran their men to earth at a temporary accommodation address. Armed with a search warrant, they made it clear that they intended to probe deeply. The two men shrugged their shoulders: what, they suggested, had they to lose by having someone else's house searched? They were only short-term tenants, bent on developing a new line of business.

In the course of their search the police came to a cupboard. It smelt earthy—which was not surprising since it contained a hundredweight or so of potatoes which had been pitched into it with the earth still clinging to them. Beneath the potatoes they found a box. Inside the box they found a tightly packed wad of £5 notes. When they had counted them, the total came to £3,999.

Questioned about them, the florist promptly answered: "They are my life's savings." And he added, spitefully: "I *work* for *my* living!"

The police were not impressed. It was unlikely that a small-time florist, working in the East End, and only now in his mid-thirties, should have amassed £4,000 by the sale of flowers and fruit. However, to be on the safe side, they checked with the bank. The numbers on the notes were examined and the bank was able to state that £3,000-worth of them had been issued only in May—the month of the robbery! The two men were therefore charged at the Central Criminal Court with stealing 600 gold bars, valued at £20,119, the property of British European Airways.

There were some surprises, however, in the course of the trial. Counsel for the Defence was able to show that the admittedly substantial sum of £3,999 in £5 notes was, in fact, the greater part of an impressive win his client had had on the racecourse! Called in evidence, a bookmaker stated on oath that he had paid over the sum of £4,775—"most of it in £5 notes," he added.

His evidence was corroborated. For a time it looked as if this successful young florist, who had so pathetically referred to his winnings as his lifetime savings, might be acquitted. Prosecuting Counsel, however, had not yet done with him. He asked the bookmaker what sort of bets the florist had made. "Credit bets, in the sums of £50, £100, £200 and £250, on various races," he answered, after reference to his book. It struck a good many people in the court that those were pretty substantial bets for anyone to make, and with this reflection in their minds, the trial was continued.

The case, however, folded suddenly. The street trader, demoralized perhaps by the slow, inexorable fashion in which information was extracted, collated and turned to a man's disadvantage, pleaded Guilty and turned Queen's Evidence. Both he and the florist whose van they had used were sentenced to longish terms of imprisonment. Only the fact that no violence had been used, the judge told them, enabled him to let them off so lightly. He may or may not have been influenced by the fact that a fifth at any rate of the sum stolen had been recovered. The gold itself, however, was not recovered; and it may be assumed that the "fence" who handled it gave very much less than its true worth to the two men who had so neatly and efficiently purloined it.

Firms responsible for the transfer of bullion ought, one would think, to have learned to beware of the movements of small vans of the type much used in and around London; particularly, perhaps, when the bullion in the process of transfer had the Swiss as consignees. For a theft of the same kind had taken place in London involving the Union Bank of Switzerland and a freight of gold worth just twice as much as the bullion lost on the Great West Road: £40,000, and less than three years before! This time, moreover, it was not B.E.A. who were concerned, but Royal Dutch Airlines—K.L.M.

Again it was towards dusk. Just before six o'clock on the evening of September 21st, 1954, a small black van of a type much used by distributors of lightweight articles in bulk, such as women's wear, turned up in a street off Theobolds Road, W.C.1, named Jockey's Fields. A petrol-pump attendant noted casually the skill with which the van was being backed down the street, but did not notice that it stopped abruptly with its rear doors close up against a larger van that was stationary at the time outside the Air Freight Depot of the K.L.M. Company. In fact, it came to a standstill so close to it that the two men who were closing the doors of their van had to step smartly on to the pavement to avoid being sandwiched.

At the instant that the black van's brakes brought it to a halt, two men leapt out of it, doubled round to the narrow gap between the two vans, reached through the still open doors and snatched at two boxes that lay on the floor. Each was about twenty inches long and six inches wide and deep, and tightly bound with strip-steel bands; together they contained just over £40,000-worth of bullion from the private gold refinery of the famous banking house of Rothschild.

The doors of the black van had swung open with the jerk of its abrupt stop. It needed only a matter of seconds, literally, for the two men to slip the two boxes from one van to the other, and tumble in after them; the engine was still running; the driver let in his clutch harshly, and the van leapt forward almost in a standing jump.

The petrol-pump attendant saw it returning up Jockey's Fields very much faster than it had entered the street. He remarked on the extraordinary verve with which it was being driven: it was shooting up the narrow street like a cork out of a champagne bottle! In a matter of seconds it had erupted into Theobalds Road and vanished round the turn with screaming tyres. And at that very instant, curiously enough, an Austin car appeared at that corner, backed somewhat clumsily across the junction and came to a standstill with its engine apparently stalled—most competently blocking the whole street!

By now, the two K.L.M. employees had, of course, raised the alarm. The police at the Gray's Inn Road station were alerted, and on the spot within a couple of minutes: the hue and cry was "on". The petrol-pump attendant had information to offer: he believed the driver had "a pale, round face, a small, dark moustache, and hair well brushed back." He was wearing, he added, a greyish sort of coat. Someone else suggested that the driver appeared to be about 38 or 40 years of age. But he was of the opinion that he was wearing "a fawn raincoat". Unhappily greyish, or fawn, raincoats, usually belted, are the standard men's wear among the smash-and-grab fraternity; and the age "38–40" is about as indeterminate as any could be.

Within an hour of the bullion robbery the black van was found: it was not a quarter of a mile from the K.L.M. Air Freight Depot; it was a van of the type used for carrying dresses between distributors and showrooms; and it was, of course, empty. The police concealed the fact that it had been discovered and left a plain-clothes man in the vicinity in the hope that someone might come along to collect it, and thus provide a clue. Meanwhile, they circulated the very vague descriptions they had collected, alerted the officials at all rail termini, ports and airports, and sent out a considerable number of plain-clothes men to have a look round the cafés, snack-bars and other rendezvous of habitual criminals, not so much in the hope of spotting a likely suspect as of ascertaining who of the "regulars" might be absent.

It was three months before they got a "lead". Early in the New Year, however, a lorry driver attracted their attention, and after a good many deep-probing inquiries he was remanded in custody at the Clerkenwell Magistrates' Court and charged with being concerned, "together with other persons not in custody", in the stealing of "eight bars of gold, valued at £40,262, being the property of Royal Dutch Airlines". Shortly afterwards, a second man was picked up by the police and also charged. Subsequently, at the Central Criminal Court, London, where, exactly a century before, to the month, Pierce, Agar, Burgess and Tester had stood their trial for a major bullion robbery and been sentenced to long periods of transportation, these two men were charged with being in receipt of money, "believed to be their share of the proceeds of a bullion robbery on September 21st by persons unknown". For their share in the robbery—which was after all no more than the crime of "receiving"—they got twelve months' imprisonment apiece. The actual thieves remained unidentified in spite of all the efforts of the police and Interpol. The £40,262 in gold bars has never been traced.

The two examples of bullion robberies hitherto mentioned are robberies "on the ground", even though air companies are concerned. Strange as it may seem, however, there are on record examples of bullion lost in transit by air. Two of them are as recent as late 1957; both of them remain unexplained.

On August 13th—obviously an unlucky date for the owners, if not for the thief, even though it was a Tuesday, not a Friday—an Air France Viscount took off from Orly Airport at 8.10 p.m., bound for Geneva. (Once again: destination Switzerland!) Part of the

Viscount's freight consisted of twelve wooden boxes, each containing gold ingots to the value of £12,500—£150,000-worth of bullion in all. When the plane touched down at Geneva and the unloading of its freight began, it was found that there were only eleven, instead of twelve, of these boxes.

Phone-calls between Geneva and Orly elicited the information that the twelve boxes had been loaded on to the plane under the supervision of two senior crew members and an armed airport policeman; the three men were prepared to state on oath that they had checked the twelve boxes jointly, both as they were being loaded into the plane and after they had been stowed on board and the tally-slip duly signed. It was pointed out that each of the boxes weighed something in the region of a hundredweight, and obviously it would require a good deal more than deft sleight-of-hand to dispose of such a bulky object under such strict supervision.

Nevertheless, the fact remained that there were only eleven boxes to be unloaded at Geneva—little more than an hour's flight from Orly. Somewhere, that twelfth box had been spirited away: it had vanished into thin, even rarefied, air! The £12,500 in gold ingots was never recovered.

Only a month or two later there was another mysterious spiriting-away of bullion, somewhere on the route between Johannesburg and Hongkong. This time the gold was valued at £10,000; but perhaps because it was lost so much further away from home than the earlier consignments, and because Hongkong has long been known as one of the happiest hunting-grounds for Black Marketeers and light-fingered gentry of many shades of off-white, yellow and brown, the loss made smaller headlines than it would otherwise have done. B.E.A., K.L.M. and Air France may even have sat back and murmured gratefully: "There, but for the grace of God . . ."

There is one known case of a major bullion loss, not through criminal act but through what are euphemistically referred to as "natural causes". It happened as long ago as 1938; and has remained an unsolved mystery for more than twenty years.

A German Lufthansa aircraft left Berlin for Milan carrying a gift from Hitler to Mussolini, his doubtful friend and ally. The gift consisted of no less than 6,000,000 marks in gold. The last message received from the plane was sent out somewhere over the Engadine region of the Swiss Alps. It gave no hint that anything was wrong; yet the plane never touched down at Milan.

A year later, some fragments of metal which appeared to have belonged to an aircraft were spotted by an Alpine guide working the Gemelli Glacier. The war intervened, and for the next ten years and more nothing further transpired. But as recently as 1954, a Frontier Guard came across some more fragments of what had unmistakably been aircraft parts. He summoned help, and in due course a party of guides discovered a number of bodies in a perfect state of preservation thanks to the everlasting ice of the region. There was evidence on some of the bodies that they had in fact been occupants of the ill-fated Lufthansa plane which had crashed sixteen years before.

As a result of this discovery, a large party of Swiss Air Police, Alpine guides and others congregated in the area and made an intensive search particularly in the Val Bregaglia region of the Engadine, south of the notorious Maloja Pass. They did find further fragments of the plane. But they found no more bodies. And they found no sign of the 6,000,000 marks in German gold known to have been on board. Glaciers the world over are receding: it is possible, even if unlikely, that some time in the future some Alpine guide or climber will be startled to see, glinting through the ancient ice, the improbable sight of frozen treasure-trove which will, on account of the rise in the value of gold today, be vastly more valuable than it was when Hitler put it on the Lufthansa plane for Mussolini.

SEVEN

Gold Smuggling

"Gold can a path through hosts of warders clear."
Horace.

THE demand for gold, and yet more gold, is so steady that there has never been any lack of gold smugglers. They may work on the grand scale, or they may be petty operators; but in either case gold is changing hands—and, of course, at a handsome profit to all concerned.

The "war" between gold smugglers and the authorities shows a pendulum-like swing, first in favour of one side, then in favour of the other—as with means of offence and defence down the ages to the present day. There is no limit to the resourcefulness of the men who wage war on the smugglers; and certainly there is no limit to the smugglers' ingenuity: for of all commodities in demand, gold can be relied upon to provide the best return on their outlay.

It may seem odd, but it is a fact that the old-fashioned device of the suitcase with the false bottom is still a favourite one with gold smugglers. Their theory is presumably that to use a suitcase is so obviously to invite suspicion that no one in his senses would adopt such a subterfuge; therefore the owner walks nonchalantly past the Customs or security officials, confident that none of them is likely to give him a second thought!

Cars, naturally, are much used these days for the illicit transfer of gold (as of other valuables such as watches, cameras and diamonds and so on). Bootleg gold has been discovered secreted in upholstery, tyres, battery-cases, petrol-tanks, and even in the transmission-system itself. Security officers seem to possess an uncanny knack of spotting the guilty car before ever they set it on one side for an exhaustive examination. Very often it is the ordinary dockside crane or the ship's own derrick that gives them their first clue.

A good example of this is the case of a car that was being slung from the quay on to the *Queen Mary*. An alert official noticed that it seemed to hang very awkwardly in its slings, and he went aboard with a colleague to have a second look at it when it had been lowered

into the hold. They looked at the tyres, but these showed no sign
that the car was in fact heavier than it should be according to its
rating. However, they had been long enough in the game to know
that it was an easy matter to pump tyres harder than their normal
pressure if there was a good reason to do so. The car stood squarely
enough on the floor of the hold, yet it had hung very awkwardly
in its slings: there was obviously a reason for this, and it was not
far to seek. The tank proved to have a false bottom, and in that
false bottom gold to the value of 300,000 dollars had been secreted!

The other *Queen* was the setting for a very similar attempt at
gold smuggling, and again it was the hoist that gave the show away
to an alert official. He knew well that the experts who loaded cars
knew how to position them so that their weight was evenly distributed; in this particular case it was a very lop-sided looking job.
He went aboard and watched the car being lowered into the hold.
When the slings were removed it settled heavily on its rear springs:
heavily enough for him to exercise his authority and have the car
immediately slung out of the hold and on to the quay for investigation. The tank was genuine all right, with no false bottom. But very
nearly two hundredweight of gold was found in ingots shaped to fit
snugly inside the inner curve of the rear bumpers and beneath the
fairing that overhung them from the bodywork!

Official records show that gold has been smuggled out of or into
countries in such diverse receptacles as hollowed-out antique
bedposts, refrigerators, the platens of typewriters, in the pages of
books skilfully hollowed out and refilled, inside violins and other
musical instruments, embedded in food packages; it has even been
found, rolled out very thin, packed between the oak or elm boards
and the inner lead lining of coffins!

Much smaller, but still very valuable, quantities of gold are
constantly being found actually on the person of travellers leaving
one country for another or crossing frontiers. It is a sad but inescapable fact that pregnant women and both men and women
suffering from some such deformity as a hunchback, frequently
come under deserved suspicion: too often has the "condition" of
the woman or the "deformity" of the apparent hunchback proved
to be the result simply of some elaborately devised garment containing illicit gold in place of mere flesh and blood!

False-bottomed footwear has always been a favourite with the
less experienced smuggler, particularly for valuables that occupy
very little space: it is a very simple matter to hollow out a heel;
or even to slit the stitching of a through-sole and insert sheets of

gold hammered out very thin. It is one of the most difficult personal smuggling devices to detect, particularly when the would-be smuggler is adept enough to match his attire.

A Customs official at an American airport once had his curiosity aroused by the manner in which a passenger walked away from the counter at which he had just presented his baggage for checking. He was obviously not drunk, yet he seemed to be teetering along, as though not fully in command of his movements. The official watched him, and his curiosity turned to suspicion immediately the man started to walk up a flight of steps. For now, the heels of his shoes, which had hitherto been almost covered by his trouser-ends, were revealed as being a good deal higher than is normal for a man's shoes. The man was followed, tactfully invited to step aside into a private room and to remove his shoes. His reluctance to do so was easily explained when it was found that in those two hollowed-out and outsize heels he had packed a very valuable quantity of purest gold dust!

Inevitably, of course, personal luggage is suspect, even when it is quite small. A woman doctor who explained that she was in a great hurry to pass through the Customs as she was bound on an urgent errand, protested strongly against having her instrument-case opened. The Customs officer had been surprised at its weight. He was less surprised when he found that, beneath a superficial layer of instruments, phials and capsules and so forth, there lay some 300 ounces of gold! This explained the fact that a small case had tipped the scales at over 25 lbs. It also explained her urgency to pass through the Customs.

The imaginativeness of the Customs officers is one of their most valuable assets. Allied to a steadily-mounting accumulation of experience, it helps to account for the entirely unexpected and indeed improbable arrests they so often make, to the great discomfiture of the hardened smuggler. One officer was curious to know why an American passenger about to board a plane for Europe should be carrying with him a substantial package of salami. It was particularly odd in view of the fact that the passenger's destination was Italy—surely the home of salami?

This officer had a useful store of those fragments of miscellaneous knowledge that come in handy at the most unexpected moments. This was one of them. He happened to know, for instance, that in warm, damp weather such as prevailed just then the odour of salami can be detected at a distance of at least twenty feet; but there was certainly no odour of salami emanating from the long, dark, well-wrapped cylinder lying on his scales and registering just over 35 lbs. weight! He took a chance, slit the outer wrapping and had a look inside. And there he found some 35 lbs. weight of pure gold, carefully rolled out in sheet form—worth more than a century's output of even the highest-quality Italian salami!

These gold smugglers, of course, are the men, so to speak, "at the end of the line". But before they can attempt to smuggle it out of the country it has in the first place to be "won"; and then probably to pass through a number of hands, at each stage leaving something worth while with the various middlemen. These are either small-time operators, or cogs in giant organizations with networks covering half the world and dealing in gold in vast quantities. Initially, however, there is the miner himself: the man who is unscrupulous enough to withhold some of the gold he mines for his employers and turn it to his own immediate advantage. The problems he raises may be seen perhaps at their best at the fabulously rich gold-fields of Ontario, Canada.

They extend for a distance of something like seven hundred miles north-west of Quebec, in the direction of Red Lake and Pickle Crow, points at which the road peters out and dog-sleds have to be used for transport. Among the most notable of the mines is the so-called Porcupine group, employing some 12,000 miners and producing about a quarter of Canada's entire annual output of gold. It has been officially estimated that gold to an annual value of no less than 4,000,000 dollars "leaks" from the Ontario gold-fields; and the men responsible in the main for this leak are the so-called "High-Graders"—men interested only in gold of a very high quality indeed.

Their organization is a complex one: a network of activity involving many types of worker, many locations, many lines of communication, conventional and otherwise. The humblest, but basically most essential, cog in their organization is the miner—one of many thousands—who works perhaps a mile underground, either alone or with a trusted mate, picking away at the yellow-flaked quartz vein that is the source of the gold: "cobbing-off", as he terms it. The vein is probably at the far end of a narrow, low-ceilinged passage; from the time he steps out of the cage at the foot of the shaft till the time he re-enters it again at the end of his shift, he may have seen no one but his mate; he will have had plenty of opportunity to "look after number one".

He cannot, of course, smuggle out of the mine any of the quartz: it is too bulky. But he can, and regularly does, operate a makeshift and astonishingly successful (and so profitable) refining-mill. It consists of no more than a short length of pipe and a steel bar just smaller than its inside diameter. Using this as a mortar-and-pestle, or stamping-mill-in-miniature, he can reduce lumps of quartz to dirt, which he throws away, and particles of fairly pure gold which it is possible, if not easy, to smuggle past the guards and security officers at the gates and various points intermediate. Once outside, he can sell his gold for very much more than the contents of his legitimate wage packet that he will collect at the end of the week: he always knows where and how to contact a purchaser of this commodity. The gold dust, if he can smuggle it out, will be worth 100 dollars to him at least.

The authorities, of course, are well aware that the individual miner is as anxious to make an income "on the side" as they themselves are to make a profit out of the mines they control. They have discovered gold being smuggled out in dinner-pails, tobacco-tins, sandwiches, cigarette-rollers, pipe-bowls, dummy penknives, half-emptied milk bottles, hollowed-out hunks of bread, cakes and pies, grapefruit and oranges, lumps of butter, dollops of jam, wedges of potted meat. They have found gold stowed inside a man's false teeth, between his toes, beneath bandages covering burns and scars, real and imaginary, in the hair of the armpits and groin, wedged inside all the natural orifices of the human anatomy; gold bulks small, and even a tiny quantity has its not inconsiderable price.

The High-Graders, whether at the mining end or among the innumerable illicit gold-refining plants, in transport, storage, delivery or export, are continuously up against a bunch of hand-picked security officers, a branch of the Canadian Police Force, known as the High-Grade Squad; these men are specialists in the detection of gold pilfering, smuggling and negotiating, and expert in the handling of awkward customers. They have their head-quarters in what is considered the centre of the gold-smuggling racket, the mining township of Timmins. From that base they operate swiftly, silently, secretly—and with shattering efficiency. They are widely respected, and feared; for they possess an uncanny flair for spotting the criminal, a doggedness in pursuit that is relentless, and a tradition as high as that of the "Mounties" themselves.

Their main activities, of course, consist in intercepting gold which is being channelled away into illegal markets: gold intercepted in bulk is obviously a better haul than an ounce or two here and there changing hands between miner and lone purchaser, even though the latter may be building up a store to sell at an enhanced price to someone with the organization necessary to transport a quantity with the minimum of risk interception. But they co-operate, too, with the mine authorities, and between them a highly organized system for the prevention of individual smuggling within the mine precincts themselves has been developed and maintained. Security measures, obviously, must have their origin in the mine itself.

All miners, on reaching the surface from the working-face, have now to pass through what they refer to as the "Dry". This is a succession of interconnected rooms. In the first, they remove all their working clothes and these are slung, in individual lockers, ceiling high. The men then walk naked to the showers, where they receive a towel and a piece of company's soap. These must be left behind them when they pass into the third room, to collect their home-going clothes. They check out, under strict supervision, after picking up their lunch-pails, which have meanwhile been subjected to a careful scrutiny for gold dust perhaps adhering to a folded scrap of butter-paper, the coffee-grounds at the bottom of a vacuum flask, and so on.

For a long time the authorities acceded to the miners' demand that they should be permitted to retain their watches even when they surrendered their lunch-pails and working clothes. The miner favoured the old-fashioned type of watch of the pattern jocularly referred to as the "turnip", and it proved a most successful method of smuggling out gold dust, and one to which the authorities did not become wise for a remarkably long while.

Their method was simple, which is probably why it was so efficient. It involved close co-operation between a miner and his mate, a certain degree of skill in sleight-of-hand, and two watches of identical appearance. The first miner would hang his watch on the nail provided, and take his shower. The supervisor would stroll across, pick up the watch and, if he had any reason to feel suspicious, examine it, then return it to its nail. The second miner would arrive immediately afterwards, hang up his watch and prepare to take the first miner's place beneath the shower. He, however, would pick up his mate's watch instead of his own, and depart. The supervisor might or might not examine the watch he saw on the nail; whether he did or not, it was of course a perfectly genuine watch—very different in content from the other watch, even if identical in appearance. For the first miner had taken out with him a watch containing anything up to 100 dollars-worth of gold dust, which the supervisor believed he had examined while it was on its nail. The second miner would leave the dressing-room with a genuine watch that might or might not have been examined. And once outside, they would exchange watches—and pool their very handsome resources!

This simple ruse might have continued indefinitely, but for the smartness of a supervisor more astute than most. He happened to notice that the hands on one of the watches he inspected stood at a figure which was several hours slow by true time. He knew well that no miner would be so foolish as to risk working longer than he was paid to do, so his suspicions were aroused. He opened the watch with the point of his knife—and found it packed full of semi-refined gold dust. From that day onward, no miner was allowed to retain his watch as he passed through the "Dry". The unlucky owner of the "hot", or dummy, watch had for once omitted to set the hands to tally with the exact time at which he would be passing through it, and that small oversight had been his downfall.

Gold from the "bar-and-tube" process has, of course, still to be refined considerably before it is going to be of real interest to the chief High-Graders, and this means that the gold-fields are full of illicit refineries not unlike the illicit stills in which the Irish brew their poteen. Many of these small, makeshift refineries are almost certainly known to the High-Grade Squad men, and apparently ignored, for it is in their interests, knowing that gold does leak out of the mines, to intercept it in quantity. Such refineries have been found in the open country and also in private houses, shops and offices. And the places of concealment in which the gold dust has been found are even more varied.

Semi-refined gold, for instance, has been found in hollowed-out logs stacked on sledges and being ostensibly distributed as fuel; it has been found mixed with sand and grit in the bottom of a number of big glass tanks which a citizen heatedly protested contained nothing but some tropical fish that he had bought "for the education and pleasure of my children". A member of the High-Grade Squad, off duty at the time—so far as they can ever consider themselves off duty—was once walking behind a respectably dressed, elderly woman when she suddenly checked her pace and moved awkwardly. At that moment something slipped down from inside her skirts and fell with a thud on the pavement. The "something" was a small, solid package that had proved too heavy for the tapes that had been used to suspend it from her corset; and on being opened it was found to consist of some thousands of dollars-worth of thin gold bars!

When sufficient gold has been collected, refined and brought together into manageable form, the time has come for its transfer through the next stage. The administrative branch of the High-Graders handles this part of the business, and very often a perfectly innocent—or at least apparently innocent—car owner will be co-opted.

He will be approached by some complete stranger who will suggest to him that he might care to have his car serviced "entirely without charge or obligation". All he has to do, then, is to leave his car at such-and-such a garage which specializes in overnight car-servicing. He may (or may not) be surprised to find a couple of 100-dollar bills slipped into his hand as the stranger leaves, after paying for the drinks he has ordered. They part with mutual expressions of esteem, and it is only after they have lost sight of one another (and they will not meet again) that he may perhaps wonder how this stranger knew that he was due to make a business trip to Toronto or some other town near the frontier the following day. But he has a slip of paper instructing him to take his car for further servicing at such-and-such a garage in the town to which he is going. Or he may find this address tied to the steering-wheel of his car when he collects it from the first garage the following morning.

He is not to know—or, if he does suspect, is wise not to be unduly interested—that his car will have had loaded into it in some unlikely part a package worth the whole value of his car and his own goods many times over. He may suspect; but he knows better than to dwell on his suspicions!

How often this simple scheme succeeds it is, of course, impossible even to hazard a guess. That it is still practised is proved by a recent case. One night a farmer was roused by an unusual sound and the glare of what he took to be a bonfire. Going to the window, he was horrified to see what was obviously a car furiously burning. He telephoned the police, debated whether to go and investigate, thought better of it, and retired to bed again: the highway which ran past the end of the approach-road leading to his farmstead was half a mile away, and the night was cold. If there was anyone in the car, he would either have been burnt alive, or would soon be heard hammering for help on the farmhouse door!

The police investigated, and because of what they found on the site, got in touch immediately with the High-Grade Squad. The car, a big one, was completely burnt out. Lying on the road, beside where the tyres had been, and between the axles and between the rear axle and the petrol tank, there were a number of bars of what appeared to be pure gold. The High-Grade Squad took possession of them. The assayers, after officially testing the bars for purity, set a value of 96,000 dollars upon them.

The High-Graders who loaded the gold on to the car were never caught; the owner of the car, who may or may not have been innocent of what he was carrying, never put in a claim for compensation for loss of his car—which suggests that perhaps he was not as innocent as all that! The fire had been so fierce that it was impossible to read the licence plates or even the number stamped on the engine-block. The affair remains a mystery; but it may be that the police are not over-much concerned to solve it, since they recovered the gold.

It is impossible, of course, to draw a clear-cut distinction between bullion robbery and bullion smuggling: one implies the other. When, however, the purloining of bullion is on the grand scale it is ordinarily the work of an organization whose main interest is in the removal of gold from its true owners and selling it in the highest market—which may well be in the Far East. Though the most elaborate precautions are normally taken to safeguard large quantities of bullion, it would seem that in and near the great gold-producing territories of America, and particularly of Canada, familiarity breeds an odd sort of contempt. Two episodes involving lorry drivers illustrate this excellently.

In one case the lorry driver left his vehicle in a railway siding while he had his tally-slip signed in the office a few yards away. In the other, the driver was having a quick "Coke" with a friend prior to setting off on a longish run. On each lorry, well secured to the floor and covered with heavy tarpaulin, were a number of iron-bound wooden boxes. In each case, the lorry driver emerged after a few minutes' absence to find that his vehicle had been driven away without his even hearing it. In each case the lorry was discovered not far away, abandoned—and with its load removed. The loads, however, were not recovered: a total of some 300,000 dollars-worth of gold had changed hands, thanks to someone's opportunism and someone else's casualness, in a matter of minutes! The episodes took place within a few weeks of one another; and because in that part of Canada gold seems to be looked upon about as casually as timber may be in Vancouver, or cattle on the pampas, it caused practically no stir at all!

It is well known that there are today millionaires in Canada who have come by their wealth through methods which would not bear too strict an investigation. Some of them are men who succeeded better than others in eluding the vigilance of the High-Grade Squad. They have had contacts in the world's major Black Markets in gold, which extend from central Europe to the China coast; and the prices obtained in those markets more than justify the risks they run—or allow others to run for them.

Gold which has "leaked" through the limitless ramifications of the High-Graders' organizations is referred to as "runaway" gold—an apposite name indeed. The United States of America constitute a magnificent stretch of territory for the illicit and clandestine distribution of this commodity, and the successful coups of the High-Grade Squad have revealed that the unlikeliest sort of people are intimately involved in the organizations even today. A New York "ring" which was uncovered quite recently embodied not only big business tycoons but doctors, actors, journalists, musicians, social workers, psychiatrists, theatrical producers, and even lawyers—who should surely have known better! Between them, and with their associates, they had been responsible, it was estimated, for the leakage of some 20,000,000 dollars-worth annually for several years past. Indeed, as recently as the middle '50s it was officially estimated that gold was seeping into the world's Black Markets at an annual rate of some 200,000,000 dollars-worth. And this, in spite of the fact that, technically at any rate, all U.S.A. gold is safely locked up in Fort Knox!

EIGHT

Ingots in Jeopardy

"... And Gold,
For some to keep, and some to throw away."
Alexander Pope.

THE storing of great quantities of gold—the ultimate guarantee of
a country's paper currency—naturally presents formidable problems
of security, and it is hardly surprising that the Bank of England, the
Banque de France and other great banks are a little coy about
publishing details of their methods of safeguarding their treasure.
The United States Treasury is a little more forthcoming on the
matter: which is curious, since by far the greatest hoard of gold in
the world today—and for the foreseeable future—lies in its Bullion
Depository at Fort Knox, some thirty miles from Louisville,
Kentucky. The gold stored there, in the spring of 1959, represented
exactly £7,500,000,000! And we know more than a little about the
conditions in which it is stored.

In the early 'thirties the United States Government decided to
collect all the gold known to exist in all the bank vaults and elsewhere and deposit it beneath one roof. A 30,000-acre reservation in
Hardin County was appropriated for the purpose, and plans and
designs drawn up. It was a suitable location, for it lay some six
hundred miles inland from the Atlantic seaboard and was virtually
ringed by the Appalachian Mountains.

Seen from overhead—and the Treasury seems to have offered no
objection to aerial photographs!—there is an outer ring fence of
steel bars, known to be permanently electrified; within this there
is a wide, circular approach-road, with two short, straight
approaches to the massive steel-and-concrete building that encloses
the vaults. This building is 120 feet long by 105 feet wide, squat and
self-contained, with a substantial sentry-box built into each corner.
Within this is to be found the vault itself, founded on bedrock
and rising only a few yards from ground level.

In view of the fact that the quantity of gold stored there, almost
entirely in ingots, is so vast, this inner building looks absurdly small.
But it must be remembered that gold weighs extremely heavy and
occupies a ridiculously small space in relation to its value. A

contributor to the American magazine *Newsweek*, writing at the time
that this Bullion Depository was being built, commented on this,
and gave a revealing illustration of his point. A vault designed to
accommodate 6,000,000,000 dollars-worth of gold ingots—the value
believed to be stored there when the vault was first put to use—
need be no larger than a room ten yards square and ten feet high;
the size, in fact, of a garage built to accommodate a couple of
good-sized cars and a perambulator or two!

But what it lacked in size it certainly possessed in strength and
elaboration of strong-room detail. Its walls were made of steel and
reinforced concrete to a thickness of two feet and more; 750 tons
of reinforcing steel, 670 tons of steel in other forms, 4,200 cubic
yards of concrete and 2,000 cubic feet of granite, were incorporated
in the structure. The steel door to the vault weighed over twenty
tons, and its locking mechanism was so devised that no one individual knew the whole combination.

All the corridors surrounding the inner vault are fitted with
mirrors so mounted that the guards have a two-way view along
them at any single point, and are never out of sight of one another.
An elaborate system of water pipes makes it possible at a moment's
notice to flood the entire building. The vault door, and any other
point at which a would-be thief might direct oxy-acetylene or other
flame-cutting equipment, has been fitted with a secret device which
emits strong poison gas immediately heat makes contact with it.
There are photo-electric cells and other interlocking devices for
linking every point with every other point, so that the entire building
becomes "live" if an alien foot crosses the threshold. Fort Knox was
built at a cost of nearly a million dollars—and that was at the prices
in materials and labour obtaining in 1935!

Within the reservation, and linked to the vaults and surrounding
offices by telephones in duplicate and triplicate and other forms of
inter-com., a force consisting of 72 officers and 1,320 enlisted men
of the First Mechanized Cavalry is permanently on call. They are
equipped with all the necessary armament and a fleet of scout cars
and other vehicles capable of keeping them in touch with one
another and of transporting units at need from point to point in the
30,000-acre reservation.

A newspaperman who obviously possessed a sense of humour—
even a sense of the ridiculous—went to the trouble of looking up the
records of some of the earlier forms of security measures taken by the
authorities responsible for the safe custody of gold that must, from
its very nature (and that of man, also) be permanently in jeopardy.

The example he found was the depository attached to the Philadelphia Mint—one of the sources of supply of the gargantuan Fort Knox hoard; and the date was almost exactly one hundred years previously. His article quoted from the official instructions issued by the Mint:

> The Arms Chest is to contain at all times One Musket, One Bayonet, Two Pistols, and One Sword. The Chest is to be securely locked *at all times*. The Musket is to be taken out *without fail* once a month. It is then to be discharged, and *loaded anew*. The Watchman is to ring the bell in the yard *every hour* after 10.0 p.m. *Immediately thereafter*, a Watch-dog is to be led through the yard.

They ordered matters more simply, in those happy, far-off days!

And what was this gold hoard like to look at, when it had been assembled in that vault behind that 20-ton door? It consisted of many hundreds of thousands of ingots of gold, each $6\frac{3}{4}''$ long by $3\frac{1}{2}''$ wide and $1\frac{3}{4}''$ thick, weighing 400 ounces apiece, troy weight. Each of them was worth, in those days, approximately 7,000 dollars. But both their value and their numbers quickly increased: to an extent which considerably worried many of the financial experts in America at the time.

R. W. Babson, for instance, a financial statistician, used the ominous title "Gold Pot Too Big" over an article on the subject which appeared in the press not many months after the transfer of the gold to the safe keeping of Fort Knox. By dumping its entire gold reserves, then estimated at no less than 10,600,000,000 dollars, Uncle Sam, he maintained, was "putting too many eggs in one basket". For a prize so valuable, he gave warning, "Fascists or Communists may well be expected to let loose a revolution." He was, it must be remembered, writing in 1937. "The greatest step our nation has ever taken to prepare the ground for such a revolution," he ended, solemnly, "was the removal of this gold from thousands of banks, insurance companies and private individuals and placing it under the control of *one man*. The key to those great vaults is—hanging now on the wall of the President's private office!"

In fact, there was no native Fascist or Communist revolution. But within a couple of years there was a world-wide conflagration designed by one or the other body (if not both) to end in the domination of the New World and of the Old World—and their gold assets among their many other assets.

Ten years after Babson's outburst protest came from a very different quarter, and based on a very different principle. This time it was Ernest Bevin, then Foreign Secretary. "My conviction is," he said, addressing the Trades Union Congress in 1947, "that America has handicapped herself, and caused high taxation in her own country, by her failure to distribute the Fort Knox gold. She holds there the equivalent of £5,000,000,000 in gold, and *it is doing nothing*!" Today, just twelve years after he made that comment, the value of the gold held there under lock and key is exactly half as much again. With that thought in mind one may perhaps reflect on the Parable of the Ten Talents.

Almost exactly half-way between the date of Babson's protest and Bevin's comment, another vast hoard of gold was assembled in one spot; but for a very different reason, and under very different circumstances. This time the gold was British gold—to a value of £637,000,000. And what is more: it was *smuggled* gold!

The story is a strange and fascinating one that has only recently been revealed by those few who were in the know. It is a story of gold in jeopardy: such jeopardy that extraordinary methods had to be adopted for its safe keeping. And the reason? The year was 1940; France had fallen; Britain fully anticipated a Nazi invasion; if the war was to be carried on at all, then it would almost certainly have to be carried on from the Dominion of Canada. And for the successful prosecution of war—indeed, for the mere hope of existence—gold in bulk was vital.

In the summer of 1940 the Atlantic was alive with U-boats. In the month of June alone, and in the sea lanes of the North Atlantic alone, a total of 350,000 tons of Allied and neutral shipping was sunk. Yet to have the slightest chance of salvation, our gold must somehow be transferred to the comparative security of Canada—even though this involved risking its loss through U-boat activity in those vital sea lanes. It was a formidable risk that had to be taken; and the transfer of that gold, even though it was very much less in absolute value than the treasure in Fort Knox, made the operation between Philadelphia and Kentucky look, by contrast, like a children's game.

The gold was collected from all the British banks and other sources of supply and conveyed secretly to Greenock, the point of embarkation for Canada. The cruiser H.M.S. *Emerald* was selected to carry the first consignment of gold across the Atlantic, with the destroyer H.M.S. *Cossack*, of Norwegian waters and *Altmark* fame, as escort. That first consignment consisted of 2,229 wooden boxes, each containing four bars of gold; their value was in the region of £30,000,000.

So shocking was the weather on the crossing that the point came when the destroyer could not keep pace with the cruiser, and *Emerald's* captain therefore had to take the desperate decision to continue the six-days voyage without his escort. But his boldness paid off: on the seventh morning after leaving Greenock H.M.S. *Emerald* tied up at Halifax, Nova Scotia. His precious cargo was off-loaded in conditions of extreme secrecy and conveyed in a special train to Ottawa.

This, however, was only the first of a number of such consignments. One week later, a second convoy slipped unobtrusively down the Clyde and out into the North Atlantic, bound for Ottawa. This time it consisted of three liners: the *Monarch of Bermuda* and the Free Polish *Batory* and *Sobieski*; they were escorted by the battleship H.M.S. *Revenge*, the cruiser *Bonaventure* and four destroyers. Their precious freight this time consisted of no less than £192,000,000-worth of bullion—more than six times that unloaded from H.M.S. *Emerald*. The convoy sailed under the command of Admiral Sir Ernest Archer; and he knew when he sailed that in the fortnight immediately preceding his departure almost 140,000 tons of Allied shipping had been sunk in Atlantic waters.

H.M.S. *Revenge* had a main armament of eight 15-inch and twelve 6-inch guns, and a powerful auxiliary armament consisting of four batteries of 4-inch anti-aircraft guns, and their crews kept round-the-clock stations. Though it was July, the convoy encountered not only fog but icebergs; in addition, it was hampered by a breakdown in *Batory's* engine-room. Nevertheless, five days after leaving the Clyde the gold was being off-loaded at Halifax. This time the quantity was so great that no fewer than five special trains were required to transport it to Ottawa. Each train consisted of about a dozen coaches, with between 150 and 200 boxes of gold in each coach; and each train had attached to it two sleeping-coaches to accommodate the fifty security officers who worked 4-hour shifts, locked inside the coaches with the gold.

There was, of course, no gold depository in Canada comparable with that at Fort Knox. The vaults to which all this gold was consigned were those of the Bank of Canada, in Wellington Street, Ottawa. The main vault there was a chamber 100 feet long by 60 feet wide—smaller than the Fort Knox vault but adequate for this influx of gold bar and coin, with careful packing. Tens of thousands of these bars, ingots weighing approximately 27 lbs.

apiece, were methodically stacked on the floor and on specially reinforced shelving behind heavy wire mesh that reached to the ceiling.

In addition to the ingots there were no fewer than 50,000 sacks of gold coin in many different currencies. There were hundreds of thousands of gold "Napoleons" and *louis-d'or*; there were sovereigns and half-sovereigns covering many reigns; there were rare George III "spade guineas"; there were Elizabethan gold coins, gold thalers, Dutch, Scandinavian and other European gold coins of many denominations. By the time the last convoy had off-loaded its gold treasure at Halifax, and the gold trains had transported it to Ottawa, that Wellington Street bank vault housed an Aladdin's cave of riches that rivalled all the wealth that one associates with the Spanish Main, the pirates and buccaneers and privateers and other conscienceless sea rovers who built up our boyhood tales of gold and buried treasure.

This was an example of smuggling on the heroic scale; and smuggling with good cause. If all the gold ever carried by the Spaniards who had sacked the fabulous storehouses of the Incas were added to all the gold conveyed in the holds of the Armada galleons, and all this added to the sum total of the gold stolen by Morgan, Kidd, Drake and the rest of that restless fraternity, it would still look small beside the £637,000,000 in gold bar and coin that crossed the Atlantic from east to west, in danger from U-boat and mine and dive-bomber for many, many leagues, a calculated risk to ensure the survival of a nation, and through its survival the continuation of civilization as we know it. Surely the gods looked charitably upon the venture: for in the three months of the convoys, June, July and August, 1940, more than 130 Allied ships were sunk in the North Atlantic sea lanes; and not one of those was carrying gold.

Not all gold-carrying operations, however, were so successful. There was, for example, the so-called "Treasure of Dongo": a story with a beginning, a middle, but—so far—no "end".

In April, 1945, Mussolini and his mistress, Claretta Petacci, were intercepted by partisans when attempting to escape from Italy into Switzerland. They were travelling in a column of lorries containing a certain number of troops and a picked number of prominent Fascist leaders of the so-called Italian Social Republic set up by Mussolini after the 1943 armistice. On April 27th they were halted just outside the small town of Dongo, on the west bank of Lake Como at its northern end. Il Duce himself was disguised as an ordinary soldier, and he and Claretta Petacci were concealed beneath a pile of sacking and miscellaneous packages. It was not long before they were discovered, dragged out, shot dead and ignominiously hung upside down by the enraged populace of Dongo. It was one of the most sordid episodes of the whole of the final months of the Second World War.

The convoy, however, was carrying something other than Fascist leaders and soldiers. This was, in fact, gold: a hoard of bullion and coin which Mussolini was attempting to smuggle out of Italy. A reliable estimate of the value of this gold was £35,000,000, and it was assumed to be the secret funds of the Social Republic, hurriedly assembled by Mussolini so that he and his associates would not find themselves entirely penniless when they crossed the frontier into a neutral country.

That gold vanished. With the exception of a relatively small fraction of it, which the partisans subsequently admitted they used for the furtherance of what they then considered their lawful activities, the whole of this vast treasure "evaporated".

Such a situation, however, could not be allowed to persist indefinitely: that gold must be recovered. So said the authorities, and twelve years after the episode of the capture and hanging of Mussolini and Claretta Petacci the trial of those believed to be responsible for the disappearance of the Treasure of Dongo opened in the Padua Assize Court.

The delay may seem unduly great, but the fact is that a great many inquiries had to be made, and made in the face, generally, of considerable opposition. Initially there had been four partisans who openly admitted to having used some of the gold for the payment of their men; by the time the case opened, twelve years and two days later, on April 29th, 1957, the quartet had grown to three dozen and more, including a Communist Member of Parliament, Dante Gorrieri. In the course of the four months during which the trial continued, all the accused gave evidence, and no fewer than three hundred witnesses were called in to give evidence on one side or the other. Their evidence filled eight hundred pages of reportage. And, as was only to be expected, this evidence was confusing, contradictory and, on cross-examination, manifestly false or completely worthless.

The problem before the Assize Court judges was to ascertain what, in fact, did become of this vast quantity of gold. It was quickly established that it was first handed over to the commissar of the local partisan group who had waylaid the convoy and executed Mussolini. He stated on oath that he had at once had it conveyed to the strong-room of the Dongo Town Hall, and had an accurate inventory made out. He became somewhat vague, however, when he was asked to produce the inventory, or at least to state in whose hands it had been placed.

Day by day, as the case developed, certain disturbing fragments of evidence were heard. For example, only a few days after the hold-up a well-known Dongo partisan disappeared. The rumour went around that he was in fact a Fascist spy, and this was accepted by the majority. But not, however, by a girl who happened to be his fiancée. She announced publicly that she proposed to solve the mystery of his disappearance, even if it were the last thing she did. And this, in fact, was the last thing she did; for almost immediately she too disappeared from the Dongo scene. So, too, did a girl friend of hers in whom she had confided her misgivings; and shortly afterwards, the girl's father mysteriously vanished, too.

A number of conflicting theories were put forward and more or less strongly maintained—until they were disproved. Some witnesses declared that, in fact, the treasure was very much less than had been believed—a matter of a suitcase or two at most. Others declared that in the excitement of seizing Mussolini and his mistress the partisans had allowed the greater part of the convoy to escape unmolested, so that the treasure had crossed the Swiss frontier in safety. It had better be sought, they said complacently, in Switzerland; or even further afield. Who could say now, twelve years after the episode, just where all that gold might be located?

It was stated with equal positiveness that the lorry drivers had driven off at great speed, that the partisans had shot at their tyres, which had burst, and thus many of the lorries had tipped over sideways on the rough and dangerous surface of a road that was cut deep into the hill-side, and had rolled over and over all the way down to the verge of the lake. Many of them had disintegrated, they suggested, on impact with the outcrops of rock for which the district was noted; others had reached the lake and been submerged. It had not seemed worth while to the partisans to follow them and attempt salvage. After all, these witnesses said, guilelessly, how were they to know that there was anything of value aboard those lorries? And in any case, they were mainly concerned with the death and humiliation of Il Duce and Claretta Petacci.

Prosecuting Counsel was not impressed by such evidence. Particularly since he was able to call witnesses with evidence that gave the lie to much that had just been said. For example, it was well known that in many of the small farms and isolated cottages in the district surrounding Dongo there were gold coins and other pieces of gold, brought in, so the cottagers said, by children playing in the fields and exploring the crannies among the rocks. If there was a little gold, in the form of coin and bar, in the district, it was likely that there had been much more; and that someone knew where it was. The Swiss Customs officials, too, gave evidence that some years previously they had had occasion to search the baggage of a number of individuals who were attempting to cross the frontier in a suspicious manner; they had had gold in their possession in quantities unusual for persons of their type and background.

And so on. The trial continued for nearly four months: tedious, frustrating months, at the end of which the case seemed a thousand times more involved than it had been when it opened. And then, unexpectedly, in the middle of August, a juryman committed suicide! According to Italian law the presiding judge had no option but to declare the proceedings null and void. There would have to be, he announced wearily, an entirely new trial. The date of the new trial would be made known in due course. That was on August 19th, 1957. And there, for the present, the matter rests, completely inconclusive: the story of the Treasure of Dongo, allegedly worth £35,000,000, with a beginning and a middle—but no end in sight at this date!

Another vast hoard of gold came to light in an unexpected fashion; but this time it is a story with all three sections complete. Early in April, 1945, the 90th Infantry Division of the American Third Army overran a district to the south-west of Eisenach, where there is a substantial salt-mining industry. Military police engaged on checking civilian movement behind the lines stopped two German women hurrying along a minor road. They claimed that they were going in search of a midwife on behalf of a neighbour, and the military police accepted their story, which seemed genuine enough. As though in gratitude for the gesture, one of the women pointed across a field and said: "There is a salt-mine over there. And in it is all the gold in Germany."

The clue was followed up. The salt-mine proved to consist of some miles of underground passages and chambers of varying sizes, some of them open and manifestly empty, others with massive doors that were locked, barred and sealed. In one of them was found a collection of paintings by Rembrandt, Raphäel, Van Dyck and Albrecht Duerer, together with a chest containing a number of valuable manuscripts by Goethe. But, so far, no gold.

However, at the end of an apparently endless underground passage the searchers eventually came face to face with a door more massively armoured than any of the others. It resisted all attempts to open it, and finally a stick or two of gelignite had to be strategically placed and then exploded.

The door was blown neatly off its hinges. And what a sight met the eyes of the engineers as the smoke began to thin out! Canvas bags were stacked on the floor by the hundred; and each bag, when it had been opened, proved to contain ingots of gold weighing 40 lbs. apiece. There were larger sacks filled to bursting with British gold sovereigns and Italian gold 20-lire pieces; there were vast numbers of smaller canvas bags each containing a number of much smaller gold bars than the 40-lb. ingots—but pure gold all the same —some six inches long by three inches in width and almost an inch thick; there were fifty large sacks containing gold coin in the currencies of many countries: Turkish pounds, Norwegian gold crowns, American, Spanish, Portuguese and other gold coins of many denominations. In all, there were many millions of pounds' worth. If there was not, as the grateful woman had said, "all the gold in Germany", there was nevertheless a pretty substantial portion of it; and one well worth the finding!

Nor was it the only big haul made at the end of World War II. Only two months later some men of the American Third Division, their noses scenting gold, penetrated into the private cellars of the Burgomaster of Bad Gastein. Buried beneath the paved floor they found a number of massive metal-lined wooden chests and a great number of heavy canvas bags. All of these were wired and stamped with the seal of the German Legation in Berne, Switzerland. They proved to contain a great quantity of British, American and Italian gold bar and coin—to a value of more than £7,000,000. Careful investigation revealed that this treasure had for some time been concealed on Ribbentrop's estate beside Lake Fuschl, not very far from Salzburg and within view of Hitler's famous Eagle's Eyrie high above Berchtesgaden. It had been moved on his personal instructions when the advance of the Allies became too threatening.

It is unlikely, now, that other hoards of gold such as those of Mussolini and Hitler will come to light; nor, it is to be hoped, will it ever again become necessary to convey across the oceans such vast gold reserves as those which Britain dispatched in 1940 to the strong-rooms of a Canadian bank. If it does, then it will most certainly be a futile journey, a story without an end.

NINE

Buried Treasure

"Be Wise: Ignore the hoard of Gold
Once hid; 'tis better you
Make no attempt to lay your hand
On what Gods hold Taboo!"
Horace.

SUPERSTITIOUS fear has from the beginning of time been associated with the concealment of treasure, and even more so with the subsequent search for it, whether it takes place soon afterwards, or generations, even centuries afterwards. Particularly when the treasure is largely gold.

All ancient peoples and civilizations from the first regarded gold as distinct from all the other metals they knew; indeed, from all other commodities. It is not just that gold was the most valuable element in their economy; it was something that went far deeper than that: Aryans and Semites alike regarded gold as the "magic source of Life itself". The Egyptians, the Babylonians, the Indians, the Persians, all regarded gold as a "divine substance". Gold, for them, and many other communities, was a substance possessing not merely magical but sacred attributes. The Persians believed that the legendary founder of their race, Perseus, had indeed sprung from the "golden rain" that fell into the lap of Danäe, his unhappy young mother; and parallels to this deep-rooted belief may be found elsewhere in the East.

A man who possessed gold, they all believed, was a man above other men: a king, possessing the rare gift of immortality. An Egyptian Pharaoh would spend his life accumulating vast hoards of gold. But when he died, as much as possible of the gold he had acquired in his lifetime would be buried with him; it would then accompany him into the after-life, when he would achieve full and true divinity. In Mesopotamia and other regions lying further to the east, gold was just as highly valued; but there was one essential difference: a king's gold could work miracles on his behalf during his lifetime, endowing him with qualities which enabled him to transcend all other men in virtue, courage, wisdom, but he could

not take it with him into the after-life. Its magical, spiritual properties would be required by his successor.

It is for this reason that it is safe to say that the greatest hoard of
treasure ever buried in ancient or modern times belonged to a people
who spent generation after generation accumulating gold, which
brought power to a succession of their kings and leaders, and only
came to bury it when the twilight of their civilization began to
shade the Middle East, in the third century B.C. This is the Treasure
of Ecbatana. The story of the search for this treasure—a search
that has never yet succeeded and is for the time being in abeyance—
is one of superstition, fear, bravado, despair and disaster.

By the middle of the sixth century B.C. the empire of the Medes
had become so powerful that it had absorbed the whole of Assyria,
Armenia, Cappadocia and northern Mesopotamia, and almost the
whole of Persia. But in 550 B.C. Cyrus, King of Persia, rallied his
forces and with a superb effort overthrew the Median Empire.
The whole of the vast wealth that that empire had been steadily
accumulating down the centuries, from gold-bearing territory and
from the coffers of those whom they conquered, fell into Cyrus's
hands: it was his by right of conquest.

Reliable records exist of the extent of that treasure. In addition to
the vast collection of gold plate and gold ceremonial ornament,
there was the equivalent of 30,000 lbs. of gold bar. But this was no
more than the foundation of the Persians' gold hoard. First Cyrus
himself, then his successor, Cambyses, and then his successors in
turn, embarked on a tremendous campaign of gold collecting; they
aimed at erecting a superstructure of gold on this substantial gold
foundation which should outstrip all that had been known in past
centuries.

After the suicide of Cambyses, Darius I came to power and "the
treasure of the Persian Kings", as one historian puts it, "began to
assume really formidable proportions". For Darius was an outstanding organizer. One of the first things he did on attaining power
was to divide the whole of Western Asia into twenty "satrapies".
These territories were to be thoroughly explored and systematically
ransacked for gold. Large numbers of prospectors were sent out with
clear instructions either to find gold in quantity—or not return at all.
The majority of them were successful; and into the localities they
had surveyed and indicated whole armies of gold diggers were
dispatched with picks and shovels and overseers to make sure that
they did not miss a single grain of gold. Some of these armies of
miners went as far afield as the Urals and the Altai Mountains,

desolate and hazardous areas indeed. But to Darius men were expendable; all that was necessary was that they should send back the gold, for refining and ultimate storage in his capacious vaults.

To the natural hazards of these unknown territories where gold was to be won there was, so it was early reported, an additional and very terrible hazard: that of the Gryphons. To us, the gryphon may be no more than a fabulous creature alleged to have possessed two pairs of wings, the head and shoulders of a giant eagle armed with a great hooked iron beak, and the hindquarters of a lion, tapering off into a serpent's tail. To Darius's gold seekers, however, they were very real indeed; all the more so because they were the self-appointed guardians of all Western Asia's gold. They waged incessant war on the miners, tearing them to shreds with their wickedly dangerous beaks, or picking them up bodily in their great claws, then spreading their wings and soaring high over the mountains, to drop them on the jagged peaks that thrust upwards thousands of feet below.

The traditional enemies of the Gryphons were the one-eyed Arimaspians—professional stealers of gold since earliest times, according to tradition. But in the face of this new enemy, Darius's miners, the Arimaspians joined forces with their ancient enemies, and the lot of the gold miner became as grim as that of the Klondiker 2,500 years later in the story of man's unending quest for gold.

Not all the gold with which Darius was cramming his vaults came from the Urals and Altai Mountains. There was gold in the wide, slow-flowing rivers of Mesopotamia, very much nearer home. During the annual flooding of these rivers whole armies of slaves were sent to the region with enormous quantities of sheepskins. Overseers drove the slaves naked into the flood waters, where they had to stay for hours on end by day and by night with their sheepskins stretched out taut between them. The gold-bearing sand that had been washed out of the flooded banks higher upstream and was now being carried in suspension by the water would be caught in the close-curled, greasy wool.

At intervals the skins were collected, baled and sent back to Darius in great camel trains; and these would meet camel trains bringing up further supplies of skins, so that work in the Tigris and Euphrates and their subsidiaries need hardly cease. The sandy desert trails were alive, too, with caravans continuously on the move containing freights of dyed stuffs and other commodities for barter in the distant markets to which nomadic tribesmen brought gold dust for the purpose of exchange.

Herodotus, that imaginative historian, collected a wealth of curious information about this incessant gold seeking. Though he was a Greek, he was born in a city under Persian rule, and what he wrote certainly bears the stamp of authenticity, though his veracity is often called in question!

There is a race of Indians [he tells us] who are regularly employed in the procuring of gold. Near them is a desert, and in the same there are ants in size somewhat less than dogs but larger than foxes. These ants, forming their habitations underground, heap up the sand as the ants in Greece do, and in the same manner. The sand that is heaped up is mixed with gold. The Indians therefore go to the desert to get this sand, each man having three camels: on either side a male one and a female in the middle; this last, the man mounts himself, having taken care to yoke one that has been separated from her young as recently as possible; for camels are not inferior to horses in swiftness.

The Indians then set out for the gold, having first calculated the time, so as to be engaged in their plunder during the hottest part of the day, for during the great heat the ants hide themselves underground. When the Indians arrive at the spot, they fill their sacks with sand and return with all possible expedition. For the ants, immediately discovering them by the smell, pursue them, and they are equalled in swiftness by no other animal, so that if the Indians did not get the start of them while the ants were still assembling, not a man of them could be saved. Now the male camels, being inferior in speed to the females, slacken their pace; but the females, mindful of their young, do not slacken. Thus the Indians reach their homes with their gold.

It is a pleasant picture, even if one cannot entirely accept the ants, "somewhat less than dogs but larger than foxes". But by whatever means the gold was being won, it found its way eventually into the coffers and vaults of the Persian monarchs in ever-increasing quantities. The original hoard, taken from the Medes, was soon swamped, obliterated, by the vast quantities that poured in an almost unbroken stream that had its source in the territories over which the Persians now reigned supreme.

Relatively small amounts of the gold were used for ornamentation and display. It was used for the traditional golden pomegranates that were a feature of the spears with which all members of the Royal Bodyguard were armed; it was used for the stem, branches, twigs and foliage of the great ornamental tree and the wide-spreading vine that were two of the dominating features of the Royal Audience Chamber. Some of it was minted into gold coins known as "Darics".

Far and away the greatest proportion of the gold remained as bullion. This was the Royal Treasure, stored in enormous coffers, in deep vaults, but never very far from the Royal Presence. For from the possession and proximity of the gold the Persian monarch derived his omnipotence; and from his omnipotence derived the welfare and prosperity of the Persian Kingdom as a whole. The gold had, for the Persians, as for other nations which cherished it and continuously sought to augment it, a dual significance: it had both a material and a mystical value.

Darius I died; but for some two hundred years after his death his successors continued to accumulate gold in ever-increasing quantities: gold, they found—as others were to find later, and still find—begot gold. For the Persians its accumulation had become almost a religion. And among other nations their vast treasure had become a source of wonder; and of cupidity, too. Especially among the Greeks, who schemed and schemed to make it theirs.

In the latter part of the third century B.C. their opportunity came. At Arbela, near the site of ancient Nineveh, Alexander of Macedon confronted the Persian grand army, under the leadership of Darius III, and defeated him. Defeated him, even though Darius had brought the major part of the Persian gold with him as a guarantee of success in battle: for the first time in Persian history, the mystical powers of gold had betrayed one who possessed it! It was the beginning of the strange story of the fabulous Treasure of the Persian Kings "on the run"; and it illustrates the power of gold to bring trouble and disaster on those who seek to possess it.

Darius III, having lost the battle, fled eastwards, leaving his thousands of dead and dying strewn on the battlefield of Arbela, but being careful to take with him the gold, treacherous though it seemed to have been: possession of it, he thought, might yet mend his fortunes. His destination was Ecbatana, known today as Hama-dan, midway between Baghdad and the Caspian.

For some inexplicable reason, Alexander of Macedon took no immediate steps to follow him. Only months afterwards did he turn eastwards, in the tracks of Darius's great baggage-train. News of his approach reached the defeated Persian king well in advance, and by the time Alexander arrived, he had departed—it was said

for Central Asia. It was also stated in Ecbatana that he had with
him only a skeleton retinue of trusted associates.

Alexander pricked up his ears at that: if he had left so unobtrusively, clearly he could not have taken the gold with him.
Ergo, it was secreted in or near Ecbatana! Buried, no doubt; but
buried so recently that it should be easy to spot the disturbed
earth. All the available men were set to work to find the treasure
without delay; but though they searched diligently, they found
nothing.

Enraged and frustrated, Alexander went in pursuit of Darius III,
overtook him and slew him. There was no gold worth the collecting,
and he returned in heightened fury to Ecbatana to try again for
the treasure. And again without success: the gold which had failed
to rally to its owner's support was now, ironically, thwarting every
effort of the Greeks to possess it.

For centuries afterwards, the legend of buried gold in the region
of Ecbatana persisted, tantalizing all who heard it. That there was
a vast hoard of gold buried within a stone's throw of the city,
everyone knew; just where it lay concealed, no man could tell.
The astute Darius must have played his cards well. He had doubtless
had all the labourers who dug its hiding-place put to death immediately after the operation, on the recognized principle that dead
men tell no tales. On the same principle, he had doubtless put to
death those who did the slaying of the labourers. The handful of
trusty followers who carried out this grim postscript to the burial
of the gold had doubtless fled with Darius into Central Asia; the
"ten little nigger boys" were reduced by stages to "one little nigger
boy"; and he will have died with his master at Alexander's hand.

Throughout the long years of the Greek and Parthian supremacy
the legend persisted, and grew in strength as legends will. It was
strongly alive when the Roman Empire was a-building, and a
succession of Roman generals noted down the details that came
their way, with the sound idea of turning their attention to discovering the whereabouts of the gold as soon as their current campaigns
were ended. It would be an excellent means of replenishing depleted
coffers, and enriching themselves personally at the same time.

Part way through the last century B.C., three men "divided up
the world": Pompey remained in Italy, Caesar concerned himself
with Gaul, thus laying up store of unhappiness for many generations
of schoolboys, and Crassus marched eastwards into Asia, his eye
on the Persian gold that was clearly only waiting to be gathered in
by a man of enterprise and resolution. But alas for his expectations:

he became the first example (after Darius III himself) of the fashion in which bad luck overtakes seekers after hidden treasure. He was, incidentally, a contemporary of the Roman poet who warned men against laying impious hands "on what Gods hold Taboo".

Misfortune struck early. As he prepared to set out from Rome, one of his political opponents hurried to the city gate and, according to Plutarch:

Placed there a burning brazier. When Crassus arrived, he cast incense upon the flames and invoked curses which were dreadful and terrifying in themselves and were reinforced by sundry strange and dreadful gods whom he called upon by name. It was believed by all Romans that these mysterious and ancient curses possess such mighty power that no one on whom they have been brought down can hope to avoid disaster. . . .

Certainly Crassus did not. He should have heeded the warning implicit in those curses. Instead, he continued on his way to Brindisi. About to board his galley, he was accosted by an old fig seller. The figs came from the district of Caunus, which grew the most delectable figs in all Italy. "Caunus! . . . Caunus! . . ." the old man cried his wares. One of Crassus's party, more suspicious than he, or perhaps better read in Horace's *Odes*, bade him delay his voyage: "Caunus", he urged, could be interpreted as a debased dialect form of the sinister words: "*Cave ne eas!*"—"Beware, do not go!" But Crassus laughed, and went aboard his galley, spurning the fig seller.

No Roman, except one for whom the lust for gold dominated all else, would have disregarded a second warning. Crassus, however, disregarded a third. The master mariner in charge of sailing his galley respectfully submitted that in view of the change of wind it would be safest to go by the southern route, even though it was longer. Peremptorily, Crassus bade him take the northerly route, by way of Carrhae, on the direct line for Ecbatana. The skipper shrugged his shoulders; Crassus's serious-minded companion looked gloomy; and at Carrhae Nemesis caught up with this disrespectful Roman in the guise of a large Parthian army. Battle was joined, the Romans were defeated, and Crassus lost his life.

But not, as he would have hoped, in combat. Far from it. The gods, rightly insulted by his deliberate disregard of their warnings, had other plans for his death. He was captured alive; and because his captors knew well the reason for his expedition, they amused themselves by melting a quantity of pure gold in a crucible and then poured the molten gold down Crassus's throat while he still lived. It was a punishment worse by far than that which befell the unhappy Midas.

But the gods, through their mortal agents, had not done with Crassus yet. The gold-filled head was struck from his body and sent as a trophy to the Parthian king, He was about to watch a performance of Euripides's *Bacchae* given by a company of strolling players. One of the "properties" in their performance was the head of Pentheus. With a merry laugh, the Parthian king tossed Crassus's head to them, bidding them use it in place of the other, and adding that if their performance pleased him they might retain the gold that filled the mouth and throat to divide among themselves as payment for his pleasure. It was a characteristic piece of irony on the part of the gods whom Horace had urged the Romans not to displease.

Julius Caesar was the next to cast covetous eyes at the Ecbatana gold, but was stabbed to death before his plans matured. Ten years later, Mark Antony looked eastwards to a golden horizon. He set out ostensibly to avenge the defeat at Carrhae, though his true motive was a different one. He made three successive attempts, each a failure; and finally lost his life at Actium. After him, Augustus, Gaius, Germanicus, Nero and many others in the early years of the Christian era tried their luck—and had none. Disaster and death invariably followed, either directly or indirectly, sooner or later.

Fifty years after Nero's death, the Emperor Trajan organized one of the most determined and imaginative attempts to find the Ecbatana gold. He argued that so vast a treasure literally could not have been secreted in hiding-places dug by human labour. It must therefore, he reasoned, have been concealed in a river bed near Ecbatana. He decided to search the river bed. To do this he dispatched a vast army of labourers with instructions to dig a new channel for the river, then to throw a dam across and so divert the waters into the new bed they had dug for it. He would then be able to search every square foot of the old river bed at his leisure. But though his men carried out his instructions to the letter they found no hint of the Persian gold. Trajan died in A.D. 117, a disillusioned man.

In the centuries that followed there was much internecine war among the Persians, Mongols, Huns, Scythians, Turks and others, so that the region became impossible for organized gold seeking. Then came the Middle Ages, when it seems that inventive man concentrated his powers on discovering the Philosopher's Stone, to the exclusion of all other means of locating gold in bulk. Then gold was discovered in the New World, in quantities which ought' to have satisfied man's desire for it—though it certainly did not do this.

What of the future? There *must* be gold still in the neighbourhood of Ecbatana: such a vast treasure could not have been spirited away. Hoards of gold are still found; there are doubtless others yet to be found. Of which not one is likely to be comparable with that of the Persian kings. Perhaps it is now the turn of the archaeologist? What is there to prevent him from organizing a well-found expedition to comb the neighbourhood of Ecbatana for a treasure buried there 2,500 years ago? Only the solemn warning of Horace!

Would he be disheartened by that warning? Would he fear that the gods still had some tricks up their sleeves? It is unlikely. Archaeologists cannot afford to be superstitious—though there has been evidence in plenty within recent years that calamity can overtake those who search for ancient treasure even with the most upright and worthy motives! In any case, the lure of this gold is surely powerful enough to overcome any inhibitions that might momentarily be entertained by anyone whose eyes glint with the sheen of saint-seducing gold, whether ancient or near-contemporary!

Very few of the extravagant legends of great treasure hoards will stand up to scrutiny, but there is one notable exception. It concerns what is probably one of the most colossal gold hoards ever accumulated: the so-called Inca Treasure which formed the ransom of the ill-fated Inca Emperor, Atahualpa, demanded by Pizarro and his Spanish Conquistadores in 1532. The full story was superbly told by W. H. Prescott in his *History of the Conquest of Peru*. It illustrates perfectly the terrible effects on man of a lust for gold, and is particularly impressive in that the whole sordid and cruel episode resulted from a movement ostensibly prompted by religious motives: Pizarro was there to promote the cause of Christianity among what he considered to be a heathen people; he was acting under the aegis of the Holy Catholic Church.

Prescott's *History* was written after a very great deal of conscientious work, including the meticulous examination of innumerable contemporary records and the collating of a wealth of documents and other papers. He himself was a historian; he was cautious in his acceptance of stories which came his way; no one could call him gullible; he was in his fifties when he at length felt in a position to begin his great work. It is probably this impression of authenticity,

of verisimilitude, which has given so many generations of gold
seekers the desire to find for themselves the gold of which he so
persuasively writes. Even now, in the mid-twentieth century, over
a hundred years since his book was published, expeditions are fitted
out—British, Scandinavian, German, American—to locate and
take possession of this vast treasury of gold, estimated to be worth
some £250,000,000!

The cruelty and base treachery shown by Pizarro and the
Spaniards are hard to parallel anywhere in history: only the all-
obliterating passion for gold, surely, could have led men with such
a tradition of chivalry as the Spaniards had to be guilty of such
crimes.

In 1532, Pizarro captured Atahualpa, slaughtered his men—who
had come into his presence under a guarantee of safe conduct—and
demanded a ransom in gold. The setting was Caxamalca, which
appears on maps today as Cajamarca: a setting which must be
peopled by ghosts even after four hundred years.

Solid gold, insisted Pizarro. Atahualpa swept his arm round the
room in which he had been imprisoned, a room which Prescott
reliably tells us was twenty feet long, and seventeen feet wide: "I
will give you gold sufficient to cover this floor," he said. But the
Spaniard was cunning: "To what depth shall the gold lie?" he
asked. Atahualpa went over to the wall and reached to his full
height: "As high as this," he said, touching a spot on the wall
eight feet above the floor.

Pizarro, probably doubting the Inca's power to fill a space that
size with solid gold—it worked out at something like 3,500 *cubic feet*
in all—had a notary draw up a deed in legal form, having first
had a line drawn round the four walls of the room eight feet from
floor level. He felt more confident when the gold began, as
Atahualpa had promised it would, to flow in.

It arrived from every corner of the emperor's far-flung dominion.
Some of it, Prescott says, came in the form of plate weighing up to
75 lbs. apiece; gold objects arrived to a value of forty, fifty and
even sixty thousand gold pesos in a single day—and the gold peso
was worth approximately £7 at that time! Gold arrived in *cargas*—
which were a sort of litter slung on long poles so that their great
weight could be distributed among a number of carriers. One
contemporary Spanish chronicler states categorically that there
were no fewer than 100,000 of these *cargas*, each of them so heavy
that it required at least four men to lift it.

Even a mid-sixteenth-century Spaniard, surely, should have been satisfied with such a sheer bulk of gold. But possession of gold breeds desire for more, and when Pizarro realized the resources that the Incas must have at their disposal, he suddenly decided to have Atahualpa strangled. Gold was still flowing in from the outlying parts of the Inca Kingdom, but news of the emperor's death checked its flow; *cargas* were turned around, and back on their tracks went the disillusioned carriers, determined that no more gold should be fed into the Spaniards' vault at Caxamalca.

Pizarro and his associates were furious, but they realized that they had little hope of tracking down the gold that had not yet reached them, since the country was wild and dangerous and they had stirred up such anger among the Incas that nothing short of a major expedition, strongly reinforced from Spain, could hope to succeed. That there was more gold to come, he knew well: for that mark painted on the wall of Atahualpa's prison had not nearly been reached. Eventually the Conquistadores collected what gold had been delivered, set aside the customary one-fifth part for the King of Spain and divided the remainder among themselves. Then they sailed for home.

It is the gold that did *not* arrive that is known as the Inca Treasure: an estimated £250,000,000-worth in all—perhaps more! There are records in the archives of the city of Quito, and of other cities too, that this gold is buried among the mountains. And in addition to these records, there are well-authenticated stories of men, named, who came in contact with it. The story of Suarez, for instance.

Suarez was a Spaniard who settled in Quito in the latter part of the sixteenth century and employed an Indian servant named Cantuña. His business failed and he became destitute. However, he had been a generous employer, and his Indian servant told him to establish a smelting-plant in an underground chamber and he would then see what he would see. Suarez, wondering what his servant meant, did as he had been told. Meanwhile, Cantuña disappeared for a day or two. He returned at dead of night with a quantity of gold plate and gold ornaments which Suarez estimated were worth 100,000 gold pesos. It was the first of a number of such nocturnal deliveries, and the employer knew better than to badger his employee for information as to where the gold came from: there was sufficient for all his needs, and to spare.

When he died he left his property and business to his faithful servant. Cantuña was questioned by the authorities in Quito, who were not unnaturally suspicious of the turn events had taken, but he avoided their inquisition by telling them an ingenious tale of how he had sold his soul to the devil in exchange for limitless wealth! The authorities were superstitious enough to steer clear of involvement, since the devil himself was concerned, and Cantuña continued to live in prosperity until he died. Afterwards, his erstwhile employer's premises were searched and the smelting-plant discovered. But it was too late, now: they had been duped, but Cantuña had died, taking his secret with him; they were never to know where he had found the gold that had restored his master's fortunes and made his own.

There are later documents, one of which bears out the belief that a substantial part of the Inca gold was buried—and still remains buried—in Southern Ecuador. Once again, a loyal servant is involved. This time he was one of Atahualpa's men who had been employed in carrying the *cargas* of gold to Pizarro, and had turned back on hearing of their emperor's death. He fled to Lima and the Jesuits there took pity on him. When he was a very old man, being grateful for the treatment he had received from them, he revealed the secret of what he called the Quinara treasure.

Rather surprisingly the Jesuits made no attempt to follow up the information they received from him, but they did draw up an elaborate document in which details of landmarks and distances were recorded. The document eventually came into the hands of someone who, after great difficulty, succeeded in deciphering the instructions it contained. In the last years of the eighteenth century he fitted out a small expedition, penetrated into a narrow valley in the district of Guahuanga, not far from Quinara, and located a hoard of gold. It was obviously Inca gold, though, alas, it was not in anything like the quantity he had hoped to find.

But it was sufficient to interest the authorities, who had been suspicious of the inquiries he had been making in the region and had been keeping a watchful eye on him. They clamped down on him when he returned from the mountains, expropriated his gold on the grounds that it belonged to the state, and saw to it that he fitted out no more expeditions. If he had his revenge at all it must lie in the fact that the authorities who took his gold from him had to content themselves with what he had found: they found no more!

So, the saga continues, into the nineteenth and the twentieth centuries. The great bulk of this gold, which is reliably said to include life-size statues of Incas, animals in solid gold, gold plate and ornaments, gold bars and gold pesos—gold in almost literally every conceivable shape and form—still lies hidden among the Andean wilderness of Peru and Ecuador. You may stand, they say,

in Cuzco, the ancient Inca capital, in Quito, in Lima, and in several
other towns that bestride the High Andes or sprawl on their foothills,
and *smell* the Inca gold that has lain buried there for some four
hundred years. But unless some new expedition is a great deal more
fortunate than any that have preceded it, nothing more tangible
than that smell is likely to be their reward!

North of Peru, north of Ecuador, in the High Andes of Colombia,
men still talk with conviction about another vast hoard of gold,
"The Gilded Man's Gold" in Lake Guatavita. The story they tell is,
admittedly, legend; but legends often prove to be founded on fact,
and certainly this legend has persisted for centuries, and fired the
imagination and enterprise of successive generations of gold seekers.
For this is the gold of "El Dorado"—"The Gilded Man"; and it is
he who gave the name to the term so loosely used today to imply the
source of great wealth, eldorado.

The so-called Gilded Man was worshipped by a Colombian
people known as the Chibchas, one of the many communities that
fell victim to the Spaniards. An essential feature of their worship,
which was very highly organized by their priests, consisted in the
regular surrender of great quantities of purest gold, a commodity
of which these South American peoples appear to have had an
almost inexhaustible supply. The gold had to be thrown into the
waters of Lake Guatavita, beneath which, so the priests asserted,
the deity had his abode. But this was no ordinary lake; it was, in
fact, confined within the precipitous walls of an extinct volcano,
difficult of access, remote, forbidding.

Century after century, the belief has persisted that there was a
great hoard of gold beneath the waters of this lake. Only a hundred
years ago, one of the world's great explorers, Humboldt, declared
that there was gold to a value of not less than £100,000,000 within
that crater; by today's gold prices that figure would, of course, be
vastly increased. Expedition after expedition has set out in search
of that treasure, pinning their faith in the tradition of The Gilded
Man; expedition after expedition has returned from Lake
Guatavita disillusioned and, often, bankrupt.

One of the best equipped of these expeditions tried out a
technique reminiscent of much more modern engineering practice.
Having ascertained that diving was impracticable because the silt
was so fine that it was immediately stirred up and rendered the
water completely opaque, the technicians conceived the original
plan of breaching the crater wall at its thinnest part and at a level
which would mean that the entire lake automatically drained down

the outer slopes and left the lake bed dry. It was a bold plan; and what is more, it succeeded. The crater wall split and Lake Guatavita burst through it and jetted outwards in what must have been the most spectacular "tap" ever contrived by ingenious man.

The bed of the lake was revealed. When it had dried sufficiently to be walked on the engineers proceeded to drill downwards to find out its depth. They were dismayed to find that there was nearly thirty feet of sludge, and they calculated that this would entail the removal of some 30,000,000 cubic feet in all—no light task even in working conditions much less unusual than those in which they found themselves. But they had a second bright idea: this was nothing less than to breach the crater wall at intervals down the thirty feet, systematically flood the silt until it was fluid enough to drain out through each new "tap" in turn, and so persuade gravity to do their work for them!

It was an ingenious plan. In theory it would certainly work; and in practice it *ought* to have worked. But at this point it seems that the Sun God—always associated with gold—took a hand in the proceedings ,angered, perhaps, by the way in which his protégé, The Gilded Man, was having his sanctuary violated. He poured forth his rays with an intensity unusual even for Colombia—which lies athwart the Equator. The sludge was baked as hard as concrete; drill and pick broke on impact with it; the water on which the engineers relied to dilute the sludge dried up at source. And so, eventually, did the enthusiasm of the expedition. They packed up and left the £100,000,000 in gold still buried beneath 30,000,000 cubic feet of iron-hard sludge enclosed within the walls of an extinct Colombian volcano. If it is there at all, it is there still.

Less legendary and better authenticated is the story of the "Lost Dutchman Mine". This is not much more than seventy years old. But it is accompanied by such a trail of disaster and sudden death that it offers one of the best of all proofs of the well-known fact that the quest for gold inevitably brings tragedy in its train. Arizona, this time, is the setting: more narrowly, the Superstition Mountains, originally known to the Indians and Spaniards as the Sierra de la Espuma—the Mountains of Foam. They are to be found some forty miles to the east of the town of Phoenix, Arizona.

The tradition that there is gold in those mountains is an old one, and the gold mine itself was discovered by a German named Jacob Waltz, who died late in the nineteenth century, taking his secret with him to his grave. It is assumed to be the source from which Mexicans and Apache Indians derived their medium of sale and exchange. One party after another set out into the mountains to track down this source of gold, and without exception disaster followed within a very short time. Each party in turn would come upon the party that had preceded it—but only in the form of skeletons scattered at large over the trail and the rough country on either side of it; and *always* with the skulls missing! For the past seventy years and more, this has been the macabre circumstance in which prospectors have been discovered by those who went in search of them.

The story is modern enough for there to be persons living who once knew, and still remember, some of the principals in it. Two Americans recently published an account of research which they have done, spread over half a lifetime; they spoke with many who knew Jacob Waltz, who were relatives of the luckless men who vanished into the mountains so well named Superstition, and were found only as headless skeletons long afterwards. Their account is one of crossing and double-crossing, of treachery and corruption, of desperate gambling on hopeless chances; and always, in the end, of sudden death.

Year by year, even today, expeditions are still equipped and sent into the mountains in the belief that they will succeed where all others before them have failed. As recently as 1948, for instance, the *Arizona Republic*, a newspaper circulating in the very shadow of the Superstition Mountains, carried this paragraph:

Feb. 21st. The discovery of James A. Cravey, 62-year-old retired photographer of 1014, West Polk Street, Phoenix, who disappeared in the rugged Superstition Mountains last June while seeking the legendary Lost Dutchman Mine, was reported tonight by two Arizona visitors, guests at Sunset Trail Ranch, eleven miles east of here. The two men reported finding the skeleton of a man, *minus its skull*, late this afternoon while on an all-day hike in the area. Because of the hour, they did not search for the skull, but brought the man's wallet back to Sunset Trail Ranch. Identification was made through papers in the wallet. Sheriff Lynn Early, of Final County, will organize a party to pick up the skeleton tomorrow morning. Cravey is the twentieth person known to have lost his life while looking for the fabled lost mine in the Superstitions. . . .

Not long afterwards, the newspaper was able to report that the skull, too, had been found. It was lying near the head of the canyon in which the gold mine is so positively believed to be situated, and at a distance of several miles from the skeleton itself. This aroused a number of speculations: Why should the skull be so far removed from the skeleton from which it had been severed? Why should it have been chopped off at all, anyway? And by whom? Was it some lone gold miner who had murdered Cravey? Or was there a mine-working gang determined to prevent inquisitive intruders from learning its whereabouts? Was there some *ritual* involved? Why the primitive method of head-chopping, instead of the clean death by bullet?

Speculations in plenty; but conclusions were less plentiful. There were too many imponderables. But one did not need to be more than ordinarily superstitious to gain the impression that those mountains were well named, that, over and over again, the malign influence of gold was at work upon those who sought to possess themselves of it, that its traditional mysterious power worked for evil ends rather than for good.

TEN

Sunken Gold

"Wedges of Gold, great anchors, heaps of pearl,
Inestimable stones, unvalued jewels,
All scattered in the bottom of the sea. . . ."
Shakespeare.

THE United States Treasury keeps a file known as the Treasure Trove File in which an up-to-the-minute record is kept of what can be fairly called a very flourishing industry. The list of "sites" worth prospecting would appear to be endless, and their variety almost as great. The file is in unceasing demand; particularly keen is that demand when some small success somewhere has been reported by some individual or organization.

Large as America is, there seem to be few if any tracts in the whole of her 3,000,000 square miles in which it has not proved worth someone's while to prospect. In the swamps of Wisconsin, for example, a wagonload of pure gold, deliberately cached when attack from marauding Indians seemed probable, still awaits recovery. In a well-known expanse of quicksands, 350,000 dollars-worth of gold bars has lain for many years because no one has yet devised a method for successful digging in those eternally shifting sands.

But it is around the coast of America that the seeker after gold finds the most abundant choice; this is indeed a happy hunting-ground for treasure-trove. Some seekers favour the Pacific, some the Atlantic coastline. California and Florida are rivals so far as their coastal waters are concerned. Cocos Island, midway between Galapagos and Panama, on the one side, rivals the Caribbean on the other. There is room for all; and room to spare.

A well-equipped expedition not many years ago contrived to win back from Californian waters gold to the value of 190,000 dollars; on the opposite side of the continent another expedition spent some 2,000,000 dollars on dredging and salvage work—and brought to the surface 3,500,000 dollars-worth of gold—a return of nearly double their outlay. It has been estimated that off the Florida coast there remains still 170,000,000 dollars-worth of gold, simply waiting to be picked up!

And how is this enormous sum computed? Four hundred years ago the Spanish ship, *Santa Rosa*, loaded with gold paid to Cortez by the Aztec, Montezuma, estimated at 30,000,000 dollars, sank off the southernmost tip of Florida. She is now so overgrown with coral that her exact whereabouts are impossible to define. Nothing short of an atomic explosion would be likely to release her from the living grip of coral; and the damage that would result from such a drastic operation would more than outweigh the dubious benefits, for there would be few people left alive to enjoy the ill-gotten gold!

In the Gulf of Mexico, the deep water embraced by the curve of Mexico itself to the west and the State of Florida curving downwards round it to the east, there are many pirate ships lying, some of them in no great depth of water. Each of these is reasonably assumed to have bullion in her holds. The sea-bed off Cuba and other West Indian islands and the Caribbean generally must be strewn with sunken vessels whose seams are bursting with gold bars, gold plate, gold doubloons—gold, gold, gold! There was, for example, the expedition of a number of West Indian nobles bound for Spain at the express invitation of the Spanish king.

Not unnaturally, they loaded aboard their vessel gifts of gold of a type and quantity in keeping with the royal command. Where the gold originally came from is a subject that need not be examined too closely, but may be easily guessed at; certainly it was unlucky gold. There was gold plate, gold coin, and gold bars so weighty and numerous that the ship's captain decided that the best policy was to remove the iron ballast he normally carried and substitute the gold: in that way, he thought, his vessel would be no heavier in the water, and would be every bit as seaworthy.

As it proved, he was right on the first count, wrong on the second. In rough weather his vessel sank; his distinguished passengers were drowned to a man; and his cargo of gold sank to the bottom of the deep blue sea, to the chagrin, no doubt, of the King of Spain. She would find herself in like company when she touched bottom, for this is the area of the sunken "plate-ships"—vessels which have carried similar valuable cargoes and have sunk, or been scuttled, with all hands and all their treseare lost. One of these plate-ships is reliably said to have had gold aboard to a value of over £2,000,000; expedition after expedition has searched for her—and been disappointed.

More recently, a Bahamian trading vessel whose official papers record that she carried "eight barrels of good red gold" was scuttled by her crew after a piece of skulduggery involving a revolt of the

Seminole Indians, organized by them on the quiet as a means of absconding with the treasure. Their plans went awry; in their panic they sank their ship; and all were losers: a not uncommon result of the corrupting influence of gold.

Tales of pirate and other gold tend to repeat themselves, and to snowball as they are passed from one to another. But the United States Treasury is concerned primarily with tales for which there is a good foundation. It is these examples of sunken gold that mainly appear on the files. There is actually a clear-cut and published tariff for treasure seekers! A man, or a syndicate, who "stakes a claim" with the Treasury knows what percentage he must pay if he is successful in recovering the gold he has obtained a permit to seek. The Treasury is in a comfortable position: if gold is recovered, a generous percentage automatically comes its way; if the attempt at recovery fails, the loss is entirely that of the man, or syndicate, who applied for the permit. It is a case of "Heads I win, tails you lose!"

Many of the sites where gold is reputed to lie are remote and difficult of access, expensive to work. Not all of them, however, by any means. On the U.S. Treasury file there is the case of the liner *Merida* which foundered off Virginia not fifty years ago. She had a passenger list of wealthy refugees and gold on board to a declared value of 5,000,000 dollars. There has been a steady succession of attempts to locate the liner and recover her gold, but every one of them so far has ignominiously failed.

Probably the strangest of all these properly authenticated examples of sunken gold is also the one nearest to the working heart of the United States, New York. Indeed, it may truly be said to be literally on every New Yorker's doorstep. The site is close to what is today 135th Street, within some eight miles of the dead centre of the city. But it happens also to be the bed of the East River!

Here, in 1780, the British man-o'-war H.M.S. *Hussar*, carrying gold for the wages of British troops fighting in the American Revolution, struck a reef and sank in twelve fathoms. Many of her crew were saved; but it was impossible to save the massive chests containing 5,000,000 dollars-worth of gold sovereigns. These went to the bottom; and in spite of successive efforts to retrieve them, have remained there for a hundred-and-eighty years.

Attempts to salvage the *Hussar* were started immediately, and continued throughout many months following the disaster. It was never believed possible that a vessel her size could vanish without trace in a mere twelve fathoms.

Nevertheless, in fifty years of concentrated effort, the only trace
of the lost vessel was a Wedgwood platter which was identified as
having been part of the equipment of the Captain's saloon, a pewter
platter carrying the ship's name, and—rather more sinister—a
branding-iron of the type used for marking criminals and slaves.
Search continued throughout the nineteenth century, but nothing
more came to light.

In 1900, however, a "find" stimulated the flagging searchers to
renew their efforts. This was a heavy anchor which, when it had
been scraped of the clinging barnacles, was found to have the name
H.M.S. *Hussar* stamped on it. At least, the searchers told themselves,
we are on the site. But it was iron that they had recovered, not the
good red gold they wanted. Their enthusiasm ebbed once more.

Then Simon Lake, an engineer with an inventive turn of mind,
applied to the Treasury for a permit to start work in East River.
It was a few years before the Second World War, a century and a
half since the vessel foundered. He devised a piece of salvage equipment which he magniloquently called a "Submarine Salvager".
This consisted of a long cylinder of ample calibre, the upper end
of which was secured to the parent ship, while the lower end rested
on the river bed. A sliding door at the lower end enabled the diver to
step out on to the mud and work in comfort. When he had recovered
his gold, all he had to do, Lake explained, was to retreat into the
security of the cylinder, slide the door to behind him, and walk up
the slope to the parent ship. It was as simple as that, he said.

But apparently it was not quite so simple. Lake and his crew
spent three years on the alleged site of H.M.S. *Hussar*, just off
135th Street, before he was able to state that he had, in fact, located
the object of his search. She lay, he reported, buried now beneath
twelve feet of silt, and he reckoned that he would need a further
two years to clear this and effect an entrance into her hull. The
Treasury magnanimously renewed his permit and he set to work
with fresh enthusiasm.

During the next two years he drilled many hundreds of shafts
downwards through the silt in an attempt to outline the vessel, so
that he could then decide where to drive his main shaft that would
lead him to her bullion room. But by the time he had drilled his
thousandth shaft he had realized that the silt, kept in continuous
motion by the swift current and tide of the East River, had deepened
and indeed shifted, almost certainly taking H.M.S. *Hussar* with it.
If anything, he was further from his objective than when he had
commenced operations. Then the Second World War broke out,

and he was forced to suspend operations altogether. By then his attempts had cost him some hundreds of thousands of dollars.

H.M.S. *Hussar*, with her officially-declared cargo of 5,000,000 dollars-worth of gold in her strong-room, still lies buried in silt just off 135th Street, New York. A permit to salvage her is readily obtainable from the Department of Treasure Trove, United States Treasury. All that is necessary is unlimited funds, unlimited patience—and a measure of luck greater than that which has attended any of the many previous salvage attempts.

There is a curious parallel to the case of H.M.S. *Hussar*, again involving gold dispatched as payment in warfare. This time the gold was sent by the French Government, and it was to pay for the rebuilding and defence of Louisburg, off Nova Scotia, then under siege by the British in the Seven Years War, just a century ago. Though the exact value of the gold is not known it is certainly the equivalent of several millions of pounds sterling.

The gold brought ill-luck. Louisburg fell and it was only by a miracle that the French contrived to get the gold away before Admiral Boscawen, who was assisting the American colonists, could lay hands on it. The vessel carrying the gold sailed south-westwards down the Atlantic coastline of Nova Scotia and sought refuge in Mahone Bay, a useful hiding-place for ships since it is almost completely landlocked by a string of close-set, uninhabited islands which effectually screen it from the open water. One of the small islands is notable for a number of large oak trees, of a size unusual in that region, and takes its name from these: Oak Island.

Some thirty years after the fall of Louisburg three men were exploring the bay and its many islands, and landed on Oak Island. One of them noticed an immense oak tree of unusual appearance in that it had lettering and figures carved on its bole, and one of its major boughs cleanly sawn off. None of the other oaks bore any sign of having been interfered with by man in their centuries of growth.

Puzzling over this, one of the party noticed that the ground immediately beneath the sawn-off bough was slightly saucer-shaped, as though it had been excavated and incompletely filled in. Even more puzzled, he swarmed up the tree and out along the sawn-off bough. Near the end of this he found unmistakable evidence that rope, or possibly chain, had been slung over it. Something very heavy must have been suspended from it, too, he realized, for the bark had been deeply scored. The obvious conclusion was that block-and-tackle had been suspended from it and used to lower something to the ground—or beneath it.

Who, they asked themselves, would be likely to be slinging heavy weights from a tree trunk on a lonely, uninhabited island? The answer was obvious: a pirate; and the weight would undoubtedly be pirate gold! The saucer-like hollow in the ground was where they had filled the hole with earth to hide the treasure; all that was necessary, then, was to dig the earth away again.

After digging for some time, they ascertained that the pit was some twelve feet in diameter—evidently designed to contain a very substantial treasure! They dug on with good heart, and came to a solid "lid" of interlocked oak beams wedged into the pit sides. They soon cleared that, and dug on. Ten feet further down, they came to a second barrier of oak logs; and beyond that, to a third. They excavated to a depth of forty or fifty feet, and that involved shoring up the sides of the pit if they were not to cave in. It was becoming a major operation, and the three men had to organize a fully-fledged party to assist them, with an agreed ratio on which the gold was to be shared among them. They had, of course, no doubt whatsoever, now, that it was almost within their reach.

But it was not. Indeed, the story of their search for the buried gold makes sad reading. In the early years of the nineteenth century a depth of a hundred feet had been attained; the oak "lids" had been replaced by a succession of great stone slabs; and beneath one of these they struck water. It flowed in from some unseen spring (as they believed) so that very soon there was water to a depth of fifty feet, or nearly half the distance from the point at which they were digging and the surface far above them. Several of the men digging narrowly escaped death.

Determined not to be beaten by a spring, they decided to dig a second shaft, as close alongside as was practicable, so that the water from the main shaft would drain off into it. They dug for weeks before they reached a depth of hundred feet—only to find that their second shaft suddenly began to fill; and as rapidly as the first had done. And it was only then that it dawned on them that the water was *salt*! The discovery broke their hearts and they went home disillusioned and bankrupt.

Another syndicate was organized. Money was found to enable it to be elaborately equipped. The first stage in this new attempt was to build a number of dams across the inlets from Mahone Bay that looked as though they were responsible for the seepage of salt water into the heart of Oak Island. In 1849 a highly organized party, equipped with the most modern drilling tackle, started work on the site. The drilling rig was set up and an auger driven down to a depth of more than a hundred feet, as near the original pits as was deemed safe. The core of the drill, when examined, proved to contain fragments of heavy oak planking, a layer of clay with some metal embedded in it, more oak, more clay, more oak, and finally— a wad of clay in which glinted several gold coins! Nothing so promising had rewarded the eager searching of any previous expedition: the gold, they felt now, was virtually within their grasp; all that was needed was to bring it to the surface.

That was a hundred years ago. What gold there is, deep down in the waterlogged clay of Oak Island, remains there yet. Every successive attempt by gold seekers to dig pits that would bring them to it, or underground passages that would lead them safely from one of the pits to the original pit beneath the sawn-off oak bough, has failed. The gold buried there two hundred years ago by the French is still to be brought to the surface. May be the faces on the great *louis-d'or* smiled sardonically as the sound of the picks and spades and augers reached them through the solid, embracing earth; no doubt they will continue to smile as each successive attempt is made by men with permits in their pockets and the desire for gold warming their hearts. They keep their secret still!

There is another well-kept secret about gold whose guardian this time is, surprisingly, the ice of Antarctica. There is, too, a macabre element in this true story which singles it out from the myriad other stories of lost gold awaiting recovery.

A hundred or so years ago an Australian clipper sailed from Melbourne bound for London with a full passenger list and cargo which, according to her papers, included one ton of gold bars from the Australian gold-fields. She was the *Starry Crown*—an ill-starred vessel if ever there was one, for she vanished without trace and not one of her passengers or crew was ever heard of again.

A quarter of a century later, a Tasmanian whaler cruising among the icefloes of the Antarctic came within sight of two gigantic icebergs which, to their astonishment, had a sailing-vessel embedded between them: a full-rigged walnut held in the grip of a pair of giant nutcrackers! A search-party established the fact that this was the Melbourne clipper which had vanished without trace some twenty-five years before. One of the party, exploring below decks, came to the strong-room, which had been forced open by the ice closing in on the hull. There were chests in the strong-room, and they reminded him that the clipper was said to have sailed from Melbourne with a cargo of gold. His excitement at the discovery was tempered instantly by caution: if he kept his discovery to himself, he might be able to return later with a smaller party, and thus the individual share of the treasure-trove would be proportionately greater. Luckily for him—or, maybe, unluckily—no one else went below, and he returned to his ship without disclosing his secret to anyone. The whaler, bent on whale catching, departed quickly and never returned.

The whalerman, however, did return. As soon as opportunity came his way, he confided his secret to someone he felt he could rely on, Skipper Manton, of the *Black Dog*. They engaged the smallest crew that would be capable of handling the ship, in order to keep the gold to a restricted number, and sailed. It was an ill-starred voyage from the first. They soon ran into foul weather; pack-ice appeared long before it was anticipated; a strong wind blew the *Black Dog* off her course, into the ice, and almost before the skipper could round on his partner and upbraid him for their joint folly, his ship was trapped between two big floes, her sides stove in, and she sank before her crew could get clear. Only Manton and his partner escaped death.

They succeeded in clambering on to a sheet of ice that was unbroken, and in due course they reached the *Starry Crown*. With the last remnants of their failing strength, half-frozen and starved, they struggled on board and counted themselves fortunate to have found food there, and the means of warming themselves. Comforted, they settled in. Their prospects, they felt, might be worse: when the ice receded in the warmer weather they should be able to launch one of the ship's boats and make their way to safety; alternatively, the ship herself might be released from the icebergs in which she was at present trapped; alternatively again, they might trek back across the solid ice to the mainland, hauling provisions on a sledge, together with part at any rate of the gold: enough, certainly, to equip an expedition with which to retrieve what they had left behind them. As for the crew that had been drowned: well, their death meant a larger share of the gold for their two selves!

An ice-locked ship in the Antarctic is not an ideal situation for two men to find themselves in for any length of time. Particularly when the reason for their being in that situation is a quantity of gold within their reach, capable of being handled, weighed, counted, speculated upon, day in and day out. And sure enough, it was not very long before the presence of that gold began to exercise its traditional malign influence upon them both.

Manton suggested one day that they should split the whole of the gold into two equal shares, move it into separate cabins, one on the port side and one on the starboard, and lock their respective doors upon it. The former whaling man agreed, but thought the suggestion an absurd one in the circumstances: surely they had nothing to fear from one another? He should have known better. For only a few days later he happened to see Manton seated in his cabin with the door half open, and a loaded musket across his knees! At intervals both by day and by night he would yell to his partner that if he so much as put a foot on his side of the *Black Dog* he would blow his brains out. In sheer self-defence, the other loaded a revolver and slipped it into his belt by day and beneath his pillow by night.

Inevitably, tragedy befell. One night, the seaman, lying half asleep in his bunk, heard someone fumbling at the cabin door. It opened, and in the dim light of a lantern in the passageway he thought he saw a man with a gun raised to his shoulder. He whipped out his revolver and fired, as he thought, over the man's head. But the intruder slumped to the floor, his gun crashing against the door jamb as he fell. The revolver bullet had gone clean through his heart!

Once more the man was alone in a wilderness of ice with gold all round him. He laboriously dug a hole in the ice and buried Manton. Then he set to work to build a sledge, knowing that if he did not make a getaway pretty soon he would go mad with loneliness and the haunting memory of what he had done. He loaded provisions on to it, and a bar or two only of the gold, for he had the wit to know that if he took any quantity of the gold it would make the sledge too heavy to haul, single-handed, over an unknown stretch of ice.

He came at length to a whaling station, already half-crazed by the loneliness of his journey and the appalling effort of dragging a sledge-load of provisions over the endless icefields. He stayed there long enough to fortify himself by a little companionship, but fearing that he might betray his secret if he stayed longer, set off once again, and eventually reached Melbourne. But by now his health and strength had cracked up and he knew that he could never make that journey again back to the ice-bound *Starry Crown*. The years went by. He gained an uncomfortable reputation for being more than a little eccentric. He had no friends. And only when he realized that he was at the point of death did he try to tell his strange story.

No one believed him, and he died without succeeding in persuading anyone that his story was true. Seen over a long period, it becomes increasingly unlikely. Nevertheless it is a story as well authenticated as any, and better than most. It may be, however,

that with the gradual warming-up of the earth and the receding of
the ice from the two Poles, that ship has at last been released by the
icebergs that confined her; her hull will have been stove in, and the
gold will no doubt have sunk into deep water, to be lost for ever.
Alternatively she may still be there. In which case perhaps the
members of some future expedition exploring in some later geo-
physical year may come across her and divert their attention
momentarily from their scientific research to the pleasurable
recovery of one ton of gold—less a couple of bars or so that were
dragged across the ice by a half-crazed whaling man years and
years ago.

It is a far cry from the Antarctic to Cocos Island, which lies to the
north of the equator in the Pacific. This island is probably the most
heavily publicized, and at the same time the most frustrating, of
all known sites of buried gold. Hardly a year passes but a new
expedition is fitted out in some part of the world, to cruise to Cocos
and win the gold that has defied so many generations of gold
seekers. Estimates of its value range as high as £100,000,000: it is
small wonder, therefore, that men are determined to gain possession
of such a treasure. Much of it is "pirate" gold; much also is Peruvian
Government gold.

The pirate Davies is said to have stowed away the whole of his
immense haul of loot on Cocos, amounting to some seven hundred
gold bars and a vast amount of coin. But another notorious pirate,
Benito Bonito, known in his day and for generations afterwards as
"Benito of the Bloody Cutlass", buried an even greater treasure
there: ill-gotten gold to a value of more than £10,000,000. It is,
however, the Peruvian Government's gold which comprises the
major part of the cache, perhaps as much as £60,000,000 worth in
all. And the circumstances in which the gold was deposited there
are not only strange but, comparatively speaking, recent.

Early in the nineteenth century it was learned that an attack on
Peru from Chile was impending. In a panic, the Peruvian Government collected a vast quantity of gold plate, life-size statues, in solid
gold, of the Twelve Apostles, a heavily-jewelled, more-than-life-size
statue of the Virgin Mary, a wealth of gold altar plate, church
vessels and other ceremonial and decorative objects all in solid
gold, and transferred the lot aboard a barquentine under the
command of a Captain Thompson. His instructions were to sail
away from Lima, and return with the treasure when things had
quietened down.

The Peruvian Government, surely, should have known better

than to put such temptation in a simple sailorman's way. But clearly they did not, for Captain Thompson sailed from Lima with all that gold, and a not unnatural, if reprehensible, determination not to return with it. Instead, he sailed due north from Lima, skirted Galapagos, Santa Cruz and San Cristobal, and in due course unloaded "eleven boatloads" of gold on Cocos Island. He had then to reflect on the handiest method of making use of this wealth that had so unexpectedly come into his possession.

While he was reflecting, Fate stepped in, true to the gold tradition. Captain Thompson's barquentine was wrecked; most of his crew were drowned, and many more of them fell into the hands of the Peruvians, who had in the meantime had their suspicions aroused and realized what had almost certainly happened. Thompson, however, they did not shoot: to kill him would mean that they had no clue as to where the stolen treasure might be! He did, however, fall ill, and used his illness to stall for time. In due course he contrived to escape from their clutches, but his illness got worse, and on his death-bed, true to tradition, he confided his secret to a friend whom he thought he could trust. One chapter had closed; another was about to begin.

His friend promptly organized a small and select company for the purposes of "general exploration", as he told them. But he did confide in one individual, a man whom he thought he could trust, the real purpose of this "general exploration". Together they designed and had made two suits of a most unusual pattern: completely lined with stout canvas pockets! When they dropped anchor off Cocos Island the two men went ashore in a small rowing-boat, "to reconnoitre".

The remainder of the crew lined the bulwarks of their vessel and watched, speculating, it may be, as to the atmosphere of secrecy which seemed to envelop the operation. They saw the two men land on the shore and walk briskly inland. And they saw them emerge not long afterwards from the trees. But this time they were walking curiously clumsily towards their rowing-boat, as though not entirely in command of their muscles. Heavily they clambered into the little boat, and prepared to manœuvre her away from the shore. The rollers were not formidable, but sufficiently massive to require skill and determination if they were to be successfully navigated. From the bulwarks the crew saw the little boat tilted upwards and over; saw the two men pitched into the water—and did not see them rise even once to the surface. "Like stones" they sank, was their comment; and had they known what was in the

stout canvas pockets of those specially tailored suits they might not
have been entirely surprised.

A second small boat was hurriedly launched, but by the time the
men reached the shore the first boat had been battered to pieces,
and the two men who had been thrown from her had completely
vanished in the fine sand beneath the waves. A public-spirited
member of the crew dived in the hope of finding them, but failed.
So far as is known, the gold that lined those pockets is the only gold
that has ever been recovered from Cocos Island; what remains is
there for the taking.

It is not, however, necessary to go so far afield in search of sunken
gold. Much nearer home, off the Dutch coast, for example, there
is a captured French frigate, the *Lutine*, which foundered one
hundred and sixty years ago with gold bars on board worth over
£1,000,000. Her bell hangs in Lloyd's of London, the world-famous
underwriters, and is tolled when a vessel is reported as definitely
known to be lost, or when a vessel previously reported "Overdue"
or "Missing" is reported safe after all. The water there is much
shallower than that of the Caribbean, but the currents and tides are
notorious, silt is carried in enormous quantities to and fro along the
coast, and though salvage operations were quickly started, the
equipment available a century and a half ago was insufficient to
raise her or extract her gold, and though a small quantity of it,
together with her bell and one or two objects such as cannon were
recovered, by now she has sunk irretrievably beneath the sea-bed
and no salvage company would feel it worth their while to attempt
her recovery.

Nearer home still, indeed, in our own home waters, a Spanish
galleon alleged to have some 17,000,000 gold pieces aboard her
sank off the Lizard. The sea there is deep and storm-swept, the
tides and currents vicious; she has never been located, her gold is
no doubt distributed widely over and beneath the sea-bed, and the
proud hull itself broken up into fragments little larger than the gold
pieces themselves. A little further north, off the Welsh coast, lies
another gold-bearing vessel, again too deeply embedded to be worth
the attempt to salvage her. She may be the Spanish galleon which
foundered in 1679 off Pembrokeshire and is believed by many to
lie in the relatively easy water of the Bristol Channel approaches.
At the time of writing a small, self-contained unit is being fitted out
with the express intention of salvaging her gold, believed to be
worth some £4,000,000. By the time these words appear in print
it may be that this expedition will have succeeded in its object.

On the analogy of other expeditions, however, it is much more likely to have failed!

The best authenticated and documented story of Spanish treasure ships in our own home waters, however, is, of course, that generally referred to as the Treasure of Tobermory. More research, both theoretical and practical, has been carried out in connection with this sunken gold than with any other in British coastal waters. The research has revealed an astonishingly large body of official documents, all of which confirm the existence of this treasure: dates are known, names are known, corroborative evidence exists in Spanish archives; only the gold remains, alas, still concealed! Though nearly four hundred years have elapsed since this galleon sank in the waters of the Inner Hebrides and countless searches have been made for the treasure she contained, Tobermory Bay holds her secret still.

What are the facts? Early in November, 1588, a galleon that was part of the great Armada that sailed from Spain to conquer England and was defeated first by the gallant "sea-dogs of Devon" and then by the elements themselves was driven to seek shelter off the Isle of Mull. She was the *Florentia*. That she reached and sheltered in Tobermory Bay is recorded in the official papers housed for anyone to see in the State Records Office in London. This is confirmed by documents preserved in the Spanish National Archives. It is also recorded that on or about November 13th the *Florentia* was scuttled and sunk in Tobermory Bay. There are references to this event in royal correspondence preserved at the Bodleian Library in Oxford.

One of these documents is a letter from the English Ambassador to the Court of Edinburgh to Queen Elizabeth. In this letter he wrote:

> The Spanish Shippe which was driven by tempest to the Ile called Mull in Maclane's Countrie is burnt, as it is here reported by Treacherie. It is thought to be one of the Principalle Shippes, verie riche and of great praie.

The person who should have been most interested in the sinking of a valuable cargo in Tobermory Bay, Isle of Mull, was the Earl of Argyll, who held the rank of Admiral of the Western Isles and to whom all wrecks in those waters belonged by royal mandate. Yet curiously enough, for some time nothing was done about the sunken Spanish ship. In due course, however, he realized what a treasure lay virtually at his sea-washed doorstep, and began to take a practical interest. But so, unfortunately for him and for the earls who succeeded him, did others. James I, for instance; and after him James II, Charles I and Charles II of England.

For many years following the sinking of the *Florentia* in Tobermory Bay there was a steady sequence of plots and counterplots, of bribery and corruption, false-witness, double-dealing and jiggery-pokery on the grand scale in which not only the Scottish nobility was involved but royalty too. Various Dukes of Argyll lost their heads on the execution-block or were imprisoned or were black-mailed into surrendering their ancient rights over territories they had ruled by royal consent for generations past. Or they were swindled out of their rights by laws swiftly passed in order to tie them hand and foot. It was a pageant of treachery and unscrupulous action of the type that seems to go hand in hand with the lust for gold.

And gold there certainly was within that sunken vessel. Spanish documents revealed that she had, in fact, been dispatched with gold on board for the wages of soldiers and sailors constituting the Armada force, and for the requirements of those who would sub-sequently have to administer the conquered territory. One of the documents referred to "30,000,000 under ye Sille of ye Gunroome". But, meanwhile, the *Florentia* lay rotting in the mud and silt just where she had been scuttled: there were, in those days, no means of investigating a wreck at such a depth, let alone salvaging her contents.

Then, almost a century after she had sunk, an enterprising Scot named Miller obtained the loan of a recently devised and highly experimental diving-bell. In this he obtained permission to descend to the sea-bed in Tobermory Bay—an extremely courageous deed since nothing of the sort had ever been attempted before. He reached the surface, having only narrowly escaped death first by suffocation and then by drowning, and reported that the galleon lay embedded in mud almost to the level of her upper deck. Her bows had been shattered by the explosion of her scuttling, but her poop seemed to be intact. His report may still be read exactly as he wrote it down: "Anent the Shippe sunk in Tippermorie in ye Sound of Mull, the Shippe being the *Fflorence of Spain*."

Nevertheless, for a century or two there were no developments. Interest had been stimulated by Miller's encouraging report, but there was no salvage equipment capable of following it up. The Argylls, and other interested parties, with or without the right to act, gnashed their teeth with frustration at having so near them so

The unassuming entrance to the greatest gold hoard of all time; the gates of the United States Gold Reserve, Fort Knox, Tennessee

Millions of pounds' worth of gold bricks formed part of the Nazi treasure found in the Reichsbank vaults, Frankfurt, in 1945

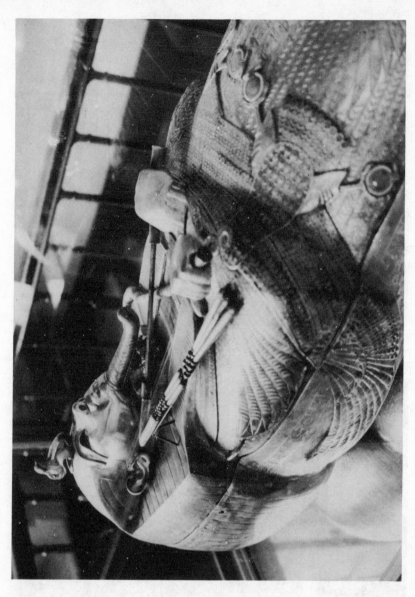

The sarcophagus
of Tutankhamen
on display at the
Cairo Museum

desirable and yet so inaccessible a treasure; the ancient rights over wrecks in Hebridean waters were won back after long and bitter struggles, but these cherished rights brought no one any nearer to his desires.

Some three hundred years after the sinking of the *Florentia*, however, the reigning Duke of Argyll engaged a diver equipped with new and revolutionary apparatus and set in train a determined attempt on her gold. The diver, a man named Gush, reported that the galleon was now almost completely buried beneath the silt and mud of the sea-bed which had been accumulating during three hundred years. He had probed with an iron bar and struck something resistant which he believed was not merely rock; further than that he was not prepared to commit himself. He too, like Miller, had almost lost his life, first through suffocation and then through drowning. He was not enamoured of his commission to dive for the *Florentia's* gold, in spite of the lavish promises of reward.

Disheartened, the Duke abandoned all hope of salvaging the gold, and that might well have been the end of the saga but for one Colonel Foss, who had been investigating among the documents in the State Records Office and as a result felt that it was not only ridiculous but even criminal to abandon so easily a treasure so vast. He obtained the concession from the Duke, and set to work with immense optimism as well as enthusiasm.

His efforts were to some extent successful. Shortly before the First World War he located the galleon afresh, buried now beneath six fathoms of mud and some ten fathoms of water. But the mud was of a clay-like consistency which would, he believed, greatly facilitate his men's task of excavating in it. As a result of finely co-ordinated efforts by the men below water and the crew of the parent ship, he succeeded in raising to the surface the first object ever to be salvaged from the *Florentia*, one of her guns. Then fragments of timber began to be hoisted aboard; then some cannon-balls, sent up by net; then a few pieces of good pewter plate; then some silver; then a sword blade and a number of daggers. And finally—a number of gold coins. By the end of the season, when the weather made further salvage work impossible, more than £1,000-worth of her treasure had been brought to the surface.

Then, unhappily, came the First World War and all salvage operations came to an end. When it was possible to renew them, it was found that the buoys and other markers that Colonel Foss had prudently established for this very purpose had vanished as a result of stormy weather and the movement of vessels passing among the Hebrides. He had to start all over again, and virtually from scratch.

And once again, Fate stepped in. If the divers and others working there had felt that their luck was against them when they found their marker buoys had gone, they had their belief confirmed when Colonel Foss himself, the driving-force of the whole elaborate scheme, was badly injured during pumping operations and had to be taken away to hospital for a long stretch of treatment and convalescence. Without his continued presence and encouragement the workers' enthusiasm filtered away, and before long they abandoned their task in Tobermory Bay and went elsewhere to jobs which might be less well paid but involved fewer hazards and better ultimate prospects. Colonel Foss recovered from his injuries, but he never returned to the site.

Was it, one is inclined to wonder, a half-realized superstition that made those divers and their crew abandon their labours? Did they perhaps reflect on the fact that the search for gold has so consistently been accompanied or followed by disaster? When the *Florentia* sank it was as the result of an explosion on board. This was assumed to have been deliberately brought about, but it was never established by whom. Only, it was known that a great number of Spaniards then on board lost their lives. The disaster that had overwhelmed the great Armada generally was here repeated, as it were, individually.

There had been deaths, too, among those who had staked claims on the sunken gold during more than three long centuries: many of them were innocent men who did not deserve to die, even if some of them had guilt on their hands. And now, Colonel Foss himself had narrowly escaped death, and through no fault of his own. There might (they may have argued among themselves) be further deaths to come, no man knowing who was the next to be struck down. So, they abandoned their quest for the Treasure of Tobermory, the "30,000,000 under ye Sille of ye Gunroome". Those 30,000,000 are almost certainly there to this day; but the gun-room still lies beneath many feet of mud, beneath ten fathoms of salt water. And possibly, too, beneath a curse more obstructive and dangerous to meddle with than any of the natural obstacles with which four centuries of gold seekers have had to contend.

The modern salvage worker has no time for superstition. He has a job of work to do; he has equipment worth hundreds of thousands of pounds and competent to undertake salvage work of the most exacting type; he lives in a different world from that inhabited by those early experimenters who first ventured beneath the sea with the glint of gold in their eyes. And very often his objective is as valuable as any that have lured the adventurer in the past.

For example, there is the famous case of the *Egypt's* gold. In the year 1922, this P. & O. liner was in collision with a French cargo boat off the coast of Brittany, and sank in deep water with gold in her strong-room to a value of £1,000,000. The loss was accepted as inevitable, for it was believed at that time that no diver could descend to, let alone work at, such a depth. The underwriters paid up the enormous sum for which the gold had been insured, and it was assumed that that was the end of the unfortunate matter.

However, it so happened that in the years immediately following the end of the First World War a firm of Italian salvage experts had been experimenting with a new and revolutionary device for working at depths too great for the diver to reach in any of the diving rigs customarily used. Even the massive articulated "suit of armour" that had sufficed for deep water until then would have been inadequate for depths such as those at which the Italians were experimenting. But their new device had been tried out in the tideless Mediterranean to a depth of well over fifty fathoms, and had proved completely successful.

The new apparatus consisted in the main of a massive steel diving-bell, equipped with windows, inside which the diver could be lowered by winch from the parent ship. Dangling at the end of fifty and more fathoms of steel cable, he could telephone instructions to the men on the salvage vessel who were operating a giant parrot-beaked "grab" slung from a sturdy and manœuvrable derrick: man and machine were separated by steel plating and deep water, but connected by telephone lines so that they could work as one unit.

Having demonstrated its ability to conduct salvage operations at a depth hitherto believed impracticable, this Italian firm was invited to undertake the salvaging of the *Egypt's* gold, and accepted the invitation with complete confidence; the confidence was not shared by the underwriters, but the only alternative was the dead loss of a vast sum.

Immense difficulties were involved in the operation. For this Breton coast is one of the most treacherous on the whole of the European coastline. It has a rocky wall running round much of it; there are submerged reefs as dangerous as any in the world; the water is deep; owing to the presence of the reefs and the mingling of the Channel waters with those of the Atlantic, the tides and cross-currents are notoriously difficult and unpredictable. Evidence of the long tradition of shipwreck and disaster off the coast of Brittany is to be found in the beautiful statue erected to *Notre Dame des Naufragés* on the craggy Pointe de Raz at the extreme western tip of the province: it entirely dominates the bleak, rocky, inhospitable headland and is the last object that the eyes of hundreds and thousands of drowning men have looked on before the swirling waters closed over their heads.

Recognizing the formidable difficulties confronting him, Commendatore Quaglia, the famous captain of the salvage vessel *Artiglio*, went cautiously to work. His first task was to "sweep" the whole area of sea washing the cliffs of western Brittany to locate and pin-point the wreck of the *Egypt*. This task was all the more difficult because the scattered reefs and isolated pointed rocks on the sea-bed made it impossible for him to lay his sweep hawsers on the sea-bed itself, for they would have been sheared through by the jagged edges with which they came in contact. Eventually, however, he located the sunken vessel, laid his marker buoys round her and anchored the *Artiglio* immediately overhead.

Six years had passed since the *Egypt* foundered, and a further five years passed before the salvage operation was completed. It must seem an unconscionably long time; but the difficulties and hazards really were formidable from start to finish. The periods when weather and the state of the tides made diving possible at all were short and irregular; every fresh day produced some unforeseen problem—often a series of them. The power of the water at that junction of Channel and Atlantic taxed Quaglia's equipment and apparatus to their limit. His salvage ship, *Artiglio*, was lost, and had to be replaced by *Artiglio II*. This involved the assembling and testing-out of duplicate equipment on the grand scale. His chief diver, Gianni, was lost, and before operations could be resumed he had to train an expert to take his place. The strain on his impulsive Latin temperament was as great as that on his mechanical resources.

But the time came when success marked his efforts: the diver in his steel cell had been able to direct the parrot-beaked grab through the hull of the liner and into a position in which it could snatch at and haul bodily away the steel doors of the strong-room. Once inside, it was a steady process of trial and error to extract from it the bullion chests; but one by one they were gripped and withdrawn. The gold was spilled out on the deck of *Artiglio II*: a heart-warming sight to the men who had striven after it throughout five frustrating, strenuous, dangerous seasons. It was delivered to its owners in successive consignments: £80,000-worth of bullion; 180 gold bars varying in value between £200 and £2,000 apiece; 40,000 gold sovereigns; twenty-six boxes of gold ingots; £190,000-worth of bullion; and so on.

All in all, by the time the salvage operation was wound up, Commendatore Quaglia had recovered from the sunken *Egypt* well over £732,000-worth of gold—almost three-quarters of what she had been carrying when the French cargo vessel's sharp bows rammed her amidships so that she sank in a matter of minutes. And because the price of gold in the world's markets had risen steeply in the eleven years since the disaster, a fair proportion of the gold that was not retrieved was compensated for by the increase in the price obtained for the portion that was retrieved. The operation was a triumph for the ingenious Italians; they had established an all-time record in successful deep-sea diving and salvage work, and opened a new chapter in the absorbing history of this branch of man's activities.

The problem of transporting gold in bulk from country to country becomes even more acute when the world is at war, for to the hazards of chance collision must now be added the danger of U-boats, of mines, of bombs dropped from aircraft, of interception by enemy ships. In the early months of the Second World War, for instance, R.M.S. *Niagara* struck a mine laid off the New Zealand coast when outward bound from Sydney, Australia. She sank in less than two hours, and carried to the bottom some eight tons of gold ingots, valued at the time at £2,500,000. The depth to which she sank was over seventy fathoms.

Since it was wartime, all our professional naval divers were engaged elsewhere; moreover, the Italians, who had so brilliantly succeeded in salvaging the *Egypt's* gold, were fighting on the other side; and in Australian dockyards there was no salvage equipment designed for an operation of this calibre, and at a depth of seventy fathoms. However, gold to the tune of £2,500,000 could not be allowed to vanish without a struggle: every ounce of the precious metal was invaluable in those days when munitions and man's basic needs had often to be provided by countries which demanded gold in payment and nothing else.

An Australian engineer, luckily, had followed with intense interest the whole of the *Egypt* salvage operation. Moreover, he was a man of an inventive turn of mind and he saw no reason why Australians should fail where Italians had succeeded. He announced that the firm he represented was prepared to design and construct a diving-bell on the lines of the one used on the *Artiglio*, and he declared his conviction that with this apparatus he would successfully recover the *Niagara's* gold.

While the apparatus was being constructed in the engineering shops, the operation of locating and marking the sunken vessel was begun. When she had been located, her position was marked by buoys anchored by 5-ton concrete blocks sunk all round her. Other massive blocks were sunk with steel hawsers to which the salvage vessel was connected, so that she could be maintained in position overhead in spite of the very heavy currents in the area.

At the same time, a scale-model of the *Niagara* was built from blue-prints provided by her builders. This was studied in meticulous detail by the salvage men so that they ultimately memorized every aspect of her: the idea being that they could visualize where their grab had to be placed, the obstacles it would encounter, and the best method of extricating it with, of course, successive chests of bullion in its jaws. When the diving-bell had been completed, and tested, the day came for Chief Diver Johnson to climb into it and give the order through his telephone line to "lower away".

Then began what can only be called a remote-control "blindman's buff". Dangling at the end of seventy fathoms of steel hawser, in a 3-ton steel container packed with instruments, dials, gauges, telephone mouthpieces and ear-pieces, switches for powerful lamps, Chief Diver Johnson had to direct the men operating the winches four hundred feet overhead so that they could manœuvre him into the *Niagara's* hull and give him a chance to survey the situation prior to giving them instructions on manipulating the powerful grab.

It was nine whole months before sufficient steel girders, buckled plates, bulkheads and other encumbrances had been cleared away to enable the grab to operate in the strong-room. It is not difficult to imagine the excitement the diver must have felt as, peering through one of his thick-glazed observation windows, he saw the grab lock its massive jaws on the first of the bullion chests and swing it silently away and out from the strong-room and then up through the seventy fathoms of water to the surface, momentarily lit by the ray of his powerful lamp.

When the *Niagara* sailed from Sydney she had 295 boxes in her strong-room. Each box contained two ingots, and each ingot was worth, at that time, some £4,000. There were nearly 600 of these ingots to be recovered, either in pairs still in their boxes, or, as a result of the explosion and the pressure of the deep water, singly as they lay about the strong-room floor.

The first box, containing two ingots, was seized by the grab in October, 1941. A few days later, nine boxes were successfully withdrawn from the strong-room and hoisted to the parent ship. Then there was a lengthy pause during which the weather dominated the operation and it was impossible to dive at all. In fact, the salvage job lasted for twelve months, and during those months the number of days when diving was possible at all was less than thirty; on the other days, thanks to wind, tide and cross-current, diving-bell and grab hung idly from their derricks, the diver and his crew chafing at the enforced delay.

Nevertheless, in that relatively short time, thanks to their patience and persistence, no fewer than 278 out of the original 295 ingots were successfully brought to the surface! The outstanding seventeen ingots proved inaccessible because they had broken through the strong-room floor and vanished somewhere in the remote depths of the ship. Any salvage company reckons a 50 per cent haul is a good one; in this case the percentage was nearer to 95!

The First World War, too, had its cases of gold lost and won. The most notable is that of the White Star liner *Laurentic*, which sank off Malin Head, on the north coast of Ireland, in January, 1917. She was westward bound for America with some £5,000,000-worth of gold and silver ingots on board as part payment for urgently needed munitions of war.

The depth of water in which she sank was not comparable with that in which five years later the *Egypt* was to sink; still less with that in which, during the second "war to end all wars", the *Niagara* was to sink. The British naval divers who went down to investigate found her lying in a mere twenty fathoms—less than a third of the depth of the water off the New Zealand coast in which Chief Diver Johnson had to operate. But the water off Malin Head was Atlantic water: windswept, storm-tossed, treacherous and in constant uneasy, unpredictable motion.

The *Laurentic's* gold was packed in chests weighing approximately one and a half hundredweight; nevertheless, in their first working season the divers managed to recover £500,000-worth of the gold—about one-tenth of the total value. But soon afterwards a gale of unusual ferocity sprang up and swept the whole of the north Irish coast; tides and currents were affected, and when eventually the salvage workers were able to resume operations it was found that there had been sufficient movement in the water even at twenty fathoms to slew the *Laurentic* away from her original position so violently that many of her steel bulkheads had crumpled and jammed, heavy steel girders had bent and snapped, and her whole interior had become a twisted maze of treacherous, unsuspected hazards.

In the whole of their second diving season, so appallingly difficult and dangerous had their work become that they recovered only a further £10,000-worth of the gold. They continued their operations throughout the remainder of the war and into the uneasy years of doubtful peace that followed. Logically, their work should have become easier as the months and years went by and they cleared away more and more of the structure; in fact, however, it became no easier, for the months of storm that intervened between each diving season and the next undid much of their work, further damaged the *Laurentic* and added steadily to the obstacles and hazards with which the men had to compete.

Eventually, seven years after the liner had sunk, the last diver came to the surface, for the last time. By then, out of the £5,000,000-worth of bullion that had been deposited in her strong-room, no less than £4,958,708-worth had been recovered—an extraordinarily high percentage of recovery by any standards, and considerably greater than that achieved by Johnson off the New Zealand coast. Admittedly, the depths were not comparable; but the conditions in which the *Laurentic* divers had to work off Malin Head were infinitely worse than those prevailing in New Zealand waters. It was a triumph of pertinacity, resourcefulness and courage on the part of a handful of men in quest of sunken gold.

ELEVEN

Gold from Graves

"There is gold, and a multitude of rubies."
Book of Proverbs.

"Every door is barr'd with gold, and opens but to
golden keys."
Tennyson.

THE first waves of Spanish Conquistadores who landed in the
Panama region of the New World early in the sixteenth century
did not find, as their successors were to do in Peru and Mexico
and elsewhere, monumental stone buildings and evidence of a
highly organized communal life; they found, instead, only Indians,
living in humble thatched huts. But to their surprise and certainly
to their delight they found a great wealth of gold ornaments and
objects.

In 1515, for instance, Gonzalo de Badajoz obtained from them
gold to a value estimated to have been some 200,000 dollars. An
Indian chieftain, anxious to induce the Spaniards to leave his
territory, offered as bribe "baskets of gold" to a value of 300,000
dollars. Treacherously, the Spaniards did then, as Pizarro was to
do a decade and more later: they both took their cake and ate it;
they made a token departure, carrying with them the gold they
had been given, and shortly afterwards returned in force to exact
further substantial tribute. It was a form of blackmail which they
found paid off handsomely.

Doubts are occasionally cast on the figures that are quoted in
regard to the wealth in gold of these sufferers at the hands of the
Spaniards four hundred years ago, but evidence has come to light
in recent years that in fact gold was available to them in vast
quantities. Local superstition has never doubted the wealth of the
inhabitants of the Panama region in those days: partly, it may be,
because there has never been a dearth of despoilers of graves in the
Isthmus, men who have found their illegal occupation a highly
profitable one. Their activities were always clandestine, and
heavily punished by the authorities if they became officially known.
But in 1940 permission was obtained by the Curator of the Penn-

sylvania University to lead an official expedition to a Panamanian
site believed to be of outstanding interest archaeologically.

The site was at Coclé, some seventy miles west of the Canal Zone
and on the Pacific slope of the mountain range. There, recent
torrential rains had swelled a river to such an extent that it had
burst its banks and carved out for itself an entirely new passage to
the coast. And in doing this, it had laid bare an extensive pre-
Columbian Indian place of burial.

The "dry" season there was short—a matter of four months at
the beginning of the year. The expedition therefore went to work
with the least possible delay, knowing that every hour was irre-
placeable. A pit some 55 feet long and 30 feet wide was excavated,
and a number of individual graves opened up at varying levels.
One of these, which the leader of the expedition assumed to be that
of a chieftain, in his own words, "fairly blazed with a wealth of
gold ornaments. The skeleton was wearing eight great gold plaques,
gold cuffs, gold armlets, several gold pendants, ear-rods, nose-clips,
sequins, small bells and 'chisels' of gold !"

The gold plaques, eight of them, varied between eight and ten
inches across and were elaborately embossed with representations
of tribal gods and sacred animals; there were also a number of
symbolic objects of great beauty, notably a crocodile in solid gold
with an emerald inset into its back, an inch in diameter. When the
gold had been subjected to tests it was found by the assayers to
be of a very high degree of purity—proof of the skill of those ancient
and allegedly simple, even primitive, people in the art of refining
the precious metal. No discovery of the kind has been made by
archaeologists in the New World that can compare with the gold
from the graves opened up in Sitio Coclé, Panama.

The gold discovered there in 1940 was not much more than four
hundred years old: its interest lay largely in the fact that so little
gold of the kind had ever been found in that continent. It is in the
Old World that one chiefly expects to find, and continues to find,
gold beautifully worked by people who lived not a mere four
hundred but three, four and more thousand years ago. Like the
gold discovered quite by chance as recently as 1947, in Azerbaijan,
between the Caspian and the Black Sea.

A shepherd boy minding his flock on a hill-side near the township
of Ziwiye happened to notice something glinting in a fissure among
some ruins that had been washed out by torrential rain. He dug
down into it, and extracted a number of metal objects, and was
peering at these, scraping the dirt from them, when a passer-by

stopped to see what he was doing. This man, a Jewish merchant, was quick to note that the metal was gold. He offered the boy a few coins in exchange for the objects, which he assured him were quite worthless. The boy, who knew a coin when he saw one, however small it might be, was well content with his bargain. And so, of course, was the Jew!

Having reached his house, he buried his treasure in the ground while he debated how best to turn it to his advantage. And that delay was his undoing. For in the meantime the shepherd boy had told his parents about his find, and what he considered his stroke of luck in exchanging it for money. His parents were at once suspicious: a Jew, they reflected, does not normally hand over coin to small boys unless there is a very good reason for doing so. They discussed the matter with others in the village and indignation was immediately generated among them: if there was profit in the possession of those objects the lad had dug out of the ground, then they saw no good reason for allowing the profit to go to the Jew. Enraged by the thought of the injustice of it all, and without reflecting that the transaction had been completed and that they themselves had no claim, they invaded the Jew's premises, beat him up, extracted by violent means the secret of where the treasure had been buried, took forcible possession of it, and departed in triumph.

It was, however, gold illegally obtained, and at once its malign influence began to work. They were too ignorant to recognize that what they held in their hands was something of immense value archaeologically and artistically; all it connoted to them was possible individual enrichment. They proceeded to quarrel as violently among themselves as they had done with the unfortunate Jew. It was only because the headman of the village exerted his authority that injury and death did not ensue. As it was, he persuaded them to break up the gold objects into as many equal parts as there were villagers, with the proviso that the lion's share came to him. The gold pieces were thereupon broken up into a great number of small and virtually worthless fragments, and each villager took home his share, to gloat over it—and of course find no profit in it for himself whatsoever!

In time the authorities got wind of what had happened and sent officials to the village to collect as many as possible of these scattered fragments. It was a tedious and frustrating task, for many of the villagers, disgusted to find that the gold was no use to them at all, had disposed of it in one way or another. Some of it had left the village and the district altogether.

When as many of them had been collected as the authorities could hope to find and obtain they were submitted to museum experts, who spent many months piecing together the often tiny, misshapen fragments—a jigsaw puzzle as valuable, perhaps, as any of which there is record. It is rare for objects of gold to be broken up so small, though glass and pottery, of course, are frequently found in almost microscopic fragments. Here, the wilful hand of man had been at work, not merely the gentler hand of Time.

When the work of restoration was completed it was found that these were indeed gold objects of priceless value. In the main they consisted of gold "pectorals"—highly ornamental breastplates, that is, designed not for the protection of the wearer in battle but for the enhancement of his dignity and prestige on ceremonial occasions: they had been, it was obvious, the personal possessions of some high dignitary, maybe a chieftain or a prince.

All were of solid gold. They were beautifully and skilfully engraved, embossed, and chiselled with designs incorporating the Tree-of-Life motif and the sacred ibex. The gryphon, too, was much in evidence, in a style that appeared to be a blend of the Greek and the Phoenician styles. Some of the pectorals carried magnificent embossed genie with flowing, stylized beards. There was a gold plaque that had perhaps been part of the ornamentation of a golden coffer, and there were other gold objects designed and superbly executed in the Babylonian tradition.

The Museum authorities consider that these priceless pieces of golden treasure-trove belonged originally to the Mannaeans, who were rich and powerful vassals of the Assyrians in the ninth century B.C. Their capital is known to have been called Izirtu, and it stood not far from the stronghold of the Mannaeans known in their day and for centuries afterwards as Zibie. Capital and stronghold alike were threatened in the latter part of the eighth century B.C. by Sardon II, whose armies overran and destroyed them both.

Since the finds were made among the ruins now known as Ziwiye it is assumed they were deliberately buried there, some three thousand years ago, when the Mannaeans realized that invasion was pending and might—as indeed it turned out—prove disastrous for them. They died there; and their gold, which, like the gold of Darius, had betrayed them, was lost there too. But for the chance of unusually heavy rain, and the alert eye of a shepherd boy, the gold might never have been discovered. And but for the cupidity and lust of a handful of foolish villagers, it might have been preserved for us in all its original perfection.

Incomparably the greatest find of gold in the grave, however, is, of course, that which the archaeologist Howard Carter discovered in the tomb of Tutankhamen in February, 1924. Indeed, it is hard to believe that any grave the world over will ever reveal a treasure as rich as that of the boy Pharaoh who died at the age of eighteen and was buried in the Valley of the Kings about 1400 B.C. Howard Carter's detailed story of the locating of this grave, of its opening and examination, constitutes one of the most dramatic and exciting chapters in the whole long record of Egyptology.

It was in November, 1922, that Carter uncovered an opening beneath the tomb of Rameses VI of Egypt, in the rock face above the Nile not far from Luxor, in the so-called "Valley of the Kings". No more than a glance was necessary to reveal that this was in fact a man-made opening into the solid rock: if it was there, then it was there for a purpose. Pick and shovel soon laid bare the beginning of a flight of stone steps leading downwards from the entrance. From that moment, Carter was convinced that he and his colleagues were literally on the threshold of a discovery of the first magnitude; but even he did not guess the true extent and significance of the discovery.

Archaeologists are popularly (and quite erroneously) supposed to be dry-as-dust folk, incapable of experiencing the sort of excitement that animates ordinary men and women. Carter's own words consistently give the lie to this foolish misconception. He describes how the mere realization that this flight of rock steps would almost certainly lead downwards to the tomb of a Pharaoh produced in him an excitement that was almost too great to bear:

Slowly, desperately slowly, it seemed to us as we watched, the remains of the doorway were removed, until at last we had the whole door clear before us. The decisive moment had arrived. With trembling hands I made a tiny breach in the upper left-hand corner. Darkness and blank space, as far as an iron testing-rod could reach, showed that whatever lay beyond was empty. Widening the hole a little, I inserted a candle, and peered in. At first I could see nothing, the hot air escaping from the chamber causing the candle flame to flicker. But presently, as my eyes grew accustomed to the light, details of the room within emerged slowly from the mist: strange animals, statues, and gold—everywhere the glint of gold. . . .

He goes on to speak of the sense of awe that he and his companion,

Lord Carnarvon, felt as they stood on the threshold of a discovery
which their archaeologists' instinct told them might well be without
parallel in this or any other field of excavation. The burial-chamber,
they well knew, had been hermetically sealed for more than three
thousand years. "The very air we were breathing," he says,
"unchanged throughout the centuries, we were sharing with those
who had laid the mummy to its rest. Time is annihilated by little
intimate details such as these, and—one feels an intruder."

It is not difficult to visualize them standing there together, peering
intently at what lay in the ante-chamber, now lit by powerful
electric torches that had been hurriedly brought down the steps
of the sloping passage to replace the candle they had first used.
And what, in fact, did they see?

They saw three great golden couches, the sides of which were
fashioned in the likeness of strange animals with enormously
elongated bodies and most frighteningly realistic heads. They saw
two life-size statues confronting one another against the far wall,
their stance suggesting that their role had been that of sentinels.
If they were sentinels—then what were they guarding? Almost
certainly, Carter believed, an inner chamber which would contain
the coffin of the Pharaoh himself.

These life-size statues wore kilts of gold, gold sandals, and
ornate gold head-dresses. Gold, indeed, was the keynote of this
ante-chamber. There was an ebony shrine, out of the half-open
door of which there hung a golden serpent; there was an inlaid
golden throne; there were wheels, axles, shafts and chassis of a
number of royal chariots—and even these were made of gold!
Scattered about on the floor, piled almost higgledy-piggledy, there
was an extraordinary assortment of objects, many of them impossible
to identify until they had been examined in close-up; and almost
every one of these was made of gold, many of them also being
thickly encrusted with precious stones!

In due course Carter and his colleagues penetrated the ante-
chamber and its astonishingly varied contents were carefully
removed for examination while the archaeologists themselves set
about opening up the great stone doorway which the golden
sentinels had been guarding and which bore the unbroken seals
set there when the burial-chamber itself had been hermetically
closed. When they had removed the stonework, what was their
surprise at finding their way barred by a second wall—and this time
a wall of solid gold!

It proved to be the near wall of a great golden shrine, 17 feet

long by 11 feet wide and 9 feet high. "From top to bottom," Carter
writes, "it was overlaid with gold and upon its sides there were
inlaid panels of brilliant blue faience in which were represented,
repeated over and over, the magic symbols which would ensure its
strength and safety." This shrine was surmounted by a cornice
composed of the sacred Royal Cobras and was, as he says, "the
most beautiful monument that I have ever seen".

Within this gold-plated shrine there was a second shrine, constructed of oak overlaid with gesso, and finally with gold plating
like the first shrine. Within this was a third, and even a fourth,
each one of them sheathed in heavy gold plate. The last of them,
Carter says, "had all the appearance of a golden tabernacle."
And small wonder; for it had been designed to contain the sarcophagus of the Pharaoh himself.

It was then that began the most stimulating and at the same time
the most nerve-racking period of all. Within the innermost
shrine Carter and his associates came upon a rose-granite slab,
9 feet in length by 5 feet wide. It weighed a ton. When, with
carefully manipulated block-and-tackle, they had successfully raised
this, it revealed what for three thousand years it had covered: a
sarcophagus carved from a solid block of quartzite, 9 feet long,
5 feet wide and 5 feet deep. And within the sarcophagus there lay
the golden effigy of the boy Pharaoh, 7 feet in length:

Enclasping the body of this magnificent monument [Carter
writes] are two winged goddesses, Isis and Neith, wrought in
rich gold-work upon gesso, as brilliant as the day the coffin was
made. The head and the hands of the king were "in the round",
in massive gold of the finest sculpture. The hands, crossed over
the breast, held the royal emblems—the Crook and the Flail—
encrusted with deep blue faience. The face and the features
were wonderfully wrought in sheet-gold. The eyes were of
aragonite and obsidian, the eyebrows and eyelids inlaid with
lapis lazuli.

But this was only the first surprise that awaited the archaeologists.
Beneath this coffin there was a second coffin. This contained a
second royal effigy, carved from oak and overlaid first with gesso
and then with heavy sheet-gold plating. This time the effigy
represented the deceased Pharaoh in the guise of Osiris. Again the
ornamentation on the gold plating was rich and varied: there was
red jasper, lapis lazuli and turquoise, this time. Even the framework

of the coffin itself had received "gold treatment", the massive lid being secured to it with heavy silver pins, each with an ornamental head of gold.

Possibly the archaeologists were not entirely surprised to find that a second coffin lay beneath the first, though they certainly had not expected its contents to be of such extravagance in the precious metal. They did not, however, expect to find yet a third coffin. Nevertheless, there was; and of the three coffins this was by far the most magnificent. It was over 6 feet in length and fashioned this time not of quartzite but—of solid gold!

So heavy was it that when the moment came to lift it, the combined efforts of eight men were required. Once again there was the Pharaoh's effigy, and once again it was of gold. The face and hands were highly burnished; he wore a double necklace of red and yellow gold and blue faience disc-shaped beads; the whole of the surface of the gold was incised in a richly ornamental feathered pattern; the two goddesses Nekhebet and Buto, in the form of vultures, were superimposed over the arms and abdomen of the effigy in richest *cloisonné* work inlaid with precious stones.

The solid gold lid of this coffin, which carried the effigy, was secured to the coffin itself with eight solid gold tenons. When the lid was removed, Carter and his colleagues found that below it there lay the embalmed remains of Tutankhamen himself—a beautifully preserved mummy well over three thousand years old. The mummy wore a magnificent burnished gold mask that covered not only the face but the whole of the head and shoulders too.

This mask, quite apart from its sheer value in gold, Carter held to be one of the most supremely beautiful pieces of craftsmanship he had ever seen or indeed expected to see. It was very slightly larger than life-size, fashioned of beaten and burnished gold inlaid with opaque polychrome glass, lapis lazuli, green felspar, cornelian, calcite and obsidian. On the high forehead, wrought once more in solid gold, were the royal insignia, the Vulture and the Serpent, emblems of the two kingdoms over which Tutankhamen had reigned during his short lifetime. Projecting downwards from his chin to his breast was the conventional "Beard of Osiris", again of solid gold and ornamented with lapis lazuli.

The sheer quantity of gold in the ante-chamber, the burial-chamber, and a third adjoining chamber subsequently explored by Carter was prodigious. Apart from the solid gold of the coffins and the effigies associated with them, the throne, chariots, couches, statues and other objects in the first of the chambers, and the great

Three varied examples of goldsmiths' art: (*above*) golden head-dress of a Sumerian princess (*c.* 2800 B.C.); (*below*) Renaissance salt-cellar in gold by Benvenuto Cellini (*c.* 1540); (*right*) gold cup and cover, English (1795)

Californian gold prospectors playing faro, about 1849

Mid-twentieth century casino in the Dominican Republic

shrines of the burial-chamber itself, there was an inexhaustible store of precious objects large and small, in heavy gold, often encrusted with precious stones, and all of them having some direct intimate association with the young Pharaoh.

There were ornate perfume caskets in solid gold, gold diadems inlaid with cornelian and bordered with lapis lazuli and turquoise; there were gold head fillets, gold amulets inlaid with green felspar, gold amuletic collars and pectorals of exquisite *cloisonné* work, one of these being made up of no fewer than 171 gold plaques elaborately inlaid with polychrome glass. There were innumerable bracelets, anklets, bangles and circlets, all of heavy gold inlaid with semi-precious stones; finger-rings of gold with lapis lazuli, cloudy-white chalcedony and turquoise. Tutankhamen himself was actually wearing seven massive gold bracelets on his right forearm and six on his left, and held a gold-hafted, gold-bladed dagger in a gold sheath decorated in *cloisonné* work, with his name and his many titles inscribed on it, together with an exquisitely engraved frieze depicting a scene of wild animals.

Accustomed as they were to the rich memorials of the ancient Egyptian past, Carter and his colleagues were staggered by the sheer volume of gold associated with Tutankhamen's tomb in the Valley of the Kings:

> The more one considers it [he writes] the more one is impressed by the extreme care and enormous costliness lavished by this ancient people on the enshrinement of their dead. Everywhere there is evidence of the accomplished artist and skilful craftsman. The modern observer must be astounded at the enormous labour and expense bestowed on these royal burials. Consider the carving and gilding of the shrines, the costly and intricate goldsmiths' work expended upon them, the precious metal so generously devoted to the princely dead!

It is no wonder that he and his associates were astonished by what lay revealed to them as the months of excavation proceeded. New finds continually came to light, each, they were inclined to think, more impressive in its richness and beauty than the last—save, of course, for the coffins and effigies in the burial-chamber itself. In an adjoining chamber, just when they had begun to think that the rich store of personal possessions had at last been inventoried, they came upon yet further personal belongings.

Here were objects that must have been the close and treasured

inanimate companions of the young Pharaoh during his childhood
and boyhood—he was hardly more than a boy when he died.
There were gold-plated statuettes, the heads of sacred animals
such as the serpent, in solid gold; there were canoes and Nile vessels
superbly executed in gold as perfect scale-models, some of them with
miniature golden thrones erected on them amidships. There were
the royal head-rests, in gold ornamented in faience and turquoise,
and other objects from which an almost photographically accurate
record can be built up of young Tutankhamen's private life.

These were the possessions that had surrounded him during his
boyhood years, his *lares et penates*; now that he had died, they must
travel with him to his last resting-place, so that he need not feel
cut off from the things he knew as he stepped into the unknown
world that awaited him.

Such was the known wealth of the Egyptian Pharaohs that it
is not unreasonable to assume that what was buried with Tutankhamen, valuable as it was, constituted only a fraction of the wealth
of those who reigned on the banks of the Nile during the centuries
that marked the great period in Egypt's history. In the Valley of
the Dead alone there were no fewer than twenty-seven Pharaohs
buried at one time or another. This is known, though most of their
graves have been rifled by succeeding generations of grave robbers
during the past thousands of years. The total value of the gold
that must have passed through Egyptian hands defies computation.

It may be added, though perhaps it should not be unduly stressed,
that calamity overtook the opening of Tutankhamen's tomb and
the removal of the treasures within; and death, too. The superstitious, reminding themselves that where gold is an issue disaster
must follow as the night follows day, will shake their heads; the
archaeologist, like the modern salvage worker, cannot afford the
luxury of being superstitious.

TWELVE

The Goldsmith's Art

"Like Gold to airy thinness beat. . . ."
John Donne.

THE Egyptians were using gold for ornamentation generally and
for personal adornment in particular more than 8,000 years ago.
Gold, in fact, was so common a personal possession in Egypt that a
collar of beads was the hieroglyph for the word itself. There are
wonderfully preserved wall-paintings showing figures with anklets
of gold beads; and these paintings have been dated to 6000 B.C.

These, and other, paintings are interesting, too, in that they reveal
how closely the art of the eastern goldsmith of today follows the
tradition of those earliest goldsmiths. For example, the very popular
large gold beads, unless they were to adorn royalty or the very
wealthiest of the goldsmith's clients, were most economically, as
well as skilfully, fashioned. The practice was to roll out thin sheet
into cylindrical form; the cylinder was then cut to the requisite
short length; a core of stone was then inserted to give the desired
weight and convey the impression of solidity; then the two ends
were accurately closed and sealed: to all outward appearances this
was a solid gold bead, and might therefore be sold to a customer at
gold price. It was probably one of the earliest forms of deception
practised by those of dubious integrity on those of normal
gullibility!

One of the most beautiful examples of the Egyptian goldsmith's
art in the earliest period is a set of bracelets made for the Queen
of Zer and worn by her round about the year 5400 B.C. One of these
is composed of a number of exquisitely fashioned hawks, alternately
of cast or moulded gold and of turquoise. All the hawks are of the
same size; but the gold blocks on which they stand have been
most skilfully graduated in such a way that the bracelet perfectly
fitted the royal arm for which it was made. By examining the
bracelet carefully it is possible to see by what means the goldsmith
achieved this clever graduation. He appears to have used the same
mould in every case; but into it he poured varying amounts of

gold so that the mount for each hawk differed very slightly in size from the one on each side of it.

Another of these lovely royal bracelets has for its essential feature a pattern of gold beads wrought in the form of barrel-shaped spirals not unlike those worn today on the head-dresses of the Dutch women of Rouveen and Staphorst. Their fashioning reveals an extraordinary degree of skill on the part of the Egyptian goldsmith. Each spiral is made out of gold wire hammered into a graduated thickness, so that as the spiral is developed it increases in both diameter and density and then correspondingly decreases. The spirals are linked in threes, each triplet being separated from the next by a triplet of exquisitely fashioned golden balls. Yet another of these bracelets is composed of beads of solid cast gold, each fashioned in the shape of a miniature hour-glass and separated from its neighbour by an intervening bead of amethyst.

All this shows that the earliest Egyptian goldsmiths tended to elaborate variations on gold beads of different shapes and sizes and association. But as the centuries passed they experimented more and more with other uses of gold. They evolved the gold chain, outstanding among their designs being the famous "loop-in-loop" style. They also produced an ever-growing variety of buttons, clasps and seals and small objects of intricate design and sometimes puzzling purpose: gold, for them, as for goldsmiths down the ages, was an inexhaustible challenge to their ingenuity. They learned, too, to produce gold "thread"; and this enabled them to indulge in much more delicate ornamental work, work which involved the use of gold and of precious and semi-precious stones such as the cornelian, lapis lazuli and turquoise, intricately associated.

Not all their work was on the small scale, however. Gold in Egypt was abundant—as is made clear from the wealth that was buried in Tutankhamen's tomb. A goldsmith could use it lavishly, and was only too happy to do so for a wealthy customer; and wealthy customers were not lacking.

Gold ornamentation on the massive scale became the fashion among the nobility. Heavy gold pectorals, for instance, became part of a Pharaoh's accoutrement, and pectorals only just less massive were worn by many of his high-ranking officials and closest associates. These pectorals were cast in moulds. Sometimes a full-size model of the pectoral-to-be would be made in wax and the mould then be formed round it; afterwards the whole would be heated, the wax would melt and run out through an orifice left for it, and molten gold would be run in to take its place. This method, practised by the Egyptians some thousands of years B.C., was widely adopted by goldsmiths in many countries during the centuries that followed, and has the name *cire perdue*, or "lost wax", even today. When he had removed the pectoral from the mould, the goldsmith would proceed to engrave and otherwise adorn it with such symbols, patterns and hieroglyphs as were required.

With a material as malleable as gold, as varied in its adaptability, it is small wonder that the Egyptian goldsmiths evolved more and more ways of extracting from it the beauty it possessed. During the period commonly referred to as the "Middle Kingdom", between 3500 and 3000 B.C., they evolved an entirely new method of utilizing gold for ornamentation, to be known later as "granulated" work. The granules were extremely small—each one perhaps no more than one-eighteenth of an inch in diameter! The variety of design that could be achieved in miniature with such material was limitless, and granulated work for such small objects as rings, buttons, pendants, clasps, hilts for knives and ceremonial daggers, seals and so on for a time surpassed all other forms of ornament.

It is the extraordinarily high standard of workmanship among the Egyptian goldsmiths that never fails to impress people who examine their work closely. Their attention to and love of detail for its own sake has hardly been surpassed even by the Chinese craftsmen working in their beloved ivory. They must have had inexhaustible patience and resourcefulness in the devising of detail and its perfect execution. This can be seen particularly well in the fastenings of necklets and necklaces, for example. However elaborate, beautiful, imaginative the individual beads and moulded pieces may be, time and time again it is to the locking-device, or clasp, that one turns, to satisfy once again the curiosity it first aroused.

Its workmanship is as exquisite as the pattern or device is original and imaginative. For example, a necklet may have a clasp consisting of a miniature lion's head, or perhaps a cowrie shell; in either case it will be of pure gold. But the lion's head, or shell, will have been made in two halves. In one of these there will be a beautifully tapered groove; in the other, a dovetailed tongue, so tapered that when the tongue is slipped into the open end of the groove and the necklet expanded or contracted to the right size, tongue and groove will have interlocked exactly and the golden lion's head or cowrie shell will appear, even if examined beneath a magnifying-glass, to be a single unit, without the slightest sign of a join. It is detail work such as this that persuades one that the Egyptian goldsmith worked not merely for his wage or reward, or even to enhance his local reputation, but for the sheer delight of exploiting to the full the potentialities of the material in which he worked and the individual skill which he had inherited from his forbears and developed in himself.

As the Mediterranean was the "cradle of mankind", it is not surprising that its shores were the place where the arts flourished earliest. Burial-sites in Greece and Crete and Sardinia and Cyprus and elsewhere, to say nothing of Luxor and the Valley of the Kings and other districts populated by the Egyptians, reveal specimens of the goldsmith's art which can hold their own with specimens produced many centuries later and right up to the present day. Schliemann, for instance, during his excavations at Mycenae, unearthed a magnificent hoard of objects wrought in gold which threw much light on the way of life of those who lived in the so-called "Homeric Age". Outstanding among them were two superb goblets wrought in solid gold and ornamented with exquisite reliefs depicting men and bulls, a traditional and symbolic theme.

The Greek goldsmiths, particularly in the early years when they were developing a new and borrowed art, tended to use pure gold. This they would first beat out very thin and then ornament with delicate filigree and granulated designs. It was between the sixth and the third centuries B.C. that this variant of the goldsmith's art reached its zenith, the perfection of its execution being perhaps even more remarkable than the originality of design.

It was from the Greeks that the Etruscan goldsmiths learned their trade; indeed, it takes an expert in these matters to distinguish, sometimes, between the best Greek and the best Etruscan work. The Etruscans' method of ornamentation has puzzled experts for many years, for it seems so extraordinarily complicated that for some time it was difficult to understand how they achieved their effects.

Apparently the original and extremely beautiful surface texture was produced by soldering on to a sheet of gold a vast number of microscopic grains of pure gold, these in turn often being outlined and patterned by gold wire in the most intricate convolutions. But when this gold "wire" is examined under a magnifying-glass it is found to be not a continuous piece of wire but made up of an infinite number of microscopic granules of gold, each fused to the one next to it. To the eye, this is simply "drawn" wire; under a magnifying-glass of low power it is a dotted line; strong magnification reveals the secret.

Experts in a number of countries have wondered how these

microscopic particles of pure gold were obtained. The theory that each was obtained by being cut from a lump of gold and then shaped was rejected, for clearly this process would have been so laborious that it would never have been adopted. The solution to the puzzle was, in fact, arrived at almost by accident, and it is now believed that both the Etruscans, and the Egyptians who for a period used this form of ornamentation widely, may have discovered the method in the same way.

It was found that if a largish drop of molten gold is allowed to fall from a height of about three feet on to a hard surface, instead of spreading outwards into a flat blob, as it does when dropped from a height of less than a foot, it disintegrates into a vast number of microscopic particles—into granules, in fact, almost identical with those used by the Etruscan goldsmiths. All that is necessary is a receptacle so shaped that it collects the scattered particles. These are then sorted into different sizes for use in various types of ornamentation. Some of them, the smallest, surprisingly prove to possess a mysterious buoyancy—all the more strange in that gold is such a heavy metal—that causes them to float.

Small decorative objects, such as women's hairpins, often carried small golden globes closely overlaid with these microscopic particles, which added a curiously pleasing third-dimensional quality, a decoration-in-depth, as it were, to the object so decorated, for the infinitely varying surfaces of these myriad golden granules each reflected light at a different angle.

But how were these granules attached to one another and to the surface which they adorned? It is known that the goldsmiths of ancient times had learned the use of various types of flux, including borax, nitre, pig fat, lye, wood ash, verdigris and malachite, so it is supposed that they must have adopted one or other of these in order to fuse together these innumerable particles. Benvenuto Cellini, the great medieval craftsman who wrote much about his work, used verdigris very successfully for this purpose, and it is probable that the method he used was similar to that of the Etruscans and the Egyptians before them. Modern experiments have shown that a compound of copper carbonate such as malachite, which was certainly known to the Egyptians, can be formed into a flux that can be virtually painted on to the surface to be ornamented; the gold granules can then be laid in pattern on it, and thus fused into a continuous whole. Nevertheless, extraordinary care and delicacy of touch must have been called for in order to produce these incomparably beautiful examples of true craftsmanship in gold.

Like the Etruscans, the Roman goldsmiths were influenced primarily by the Greeks, but as they developed their art they tended more and more to incorporate precious and semi-precious stones in a setting deliberately kept fairly plain though often very substantial. But as the art of the goldsmith spread throughout Europe in the early and later centuries A.D. there was, of course, a widely varied development. From the sixth and seventh centuries the goldsmith was very highly regarded, and given a social status far higher than that of most tradesmen: after all, it was his skill and artistry that lent distinction to the material possessions of the wealthy, both of the Church and in secular life.

The accent seems to have been on the monumental. Clothair, a Frankish king, for instance, is said to have ordered *two* thrones of beaten gold! Among other large objects executed in gold was the great Cross attributed to St. Eligius, which was six feet high and inlaid with mother-of-pearl mosaic; the actual cross-members were edged with lines of pearls. In the ninth century the Abbey of St. Denis was presented with a superb example of the goldsmith's art: an altar frontal in pure gold eight feet square, embossed with the figures of Christ and a number of angels and saints. The gold was further enriched with an encrustation of pearls, amethysts, garnets, sapphires and aquamarines. At about the same time, the Cathedral of St. Ambrose in Milan was presented with a gold altar frontal comparable in richness of material and beauty of design.

Not unnaturally, during the Middle Ages the commissioning of goldsmiths' work tended to remain in the hands of the Church generally, for wealth was most consistently found among the abbots and higher prelates. It is ironical to reflect that the money which went to pay for these expensive perquisites came to a large extent from the mites contributed by the hundreds and thousands of humble pilgrims who came in penitence and hope to these magnificent shrines; it was their contributions that enabled the great churchmen to patronize the goldsmiths and encourage them to develop their art.

Gradually, however, this patronage began to be shared; even tended to be wholly transferred. Now it was the great landowners who could afford to pay for objects of gold and the possession of such objects came to be, as it had been for the Assyrians, the Babylonians, the Persians, Egyptians and other ancient peoples, the outward manifestation of wealth and the concomitant power. The rich man ate off gold platters and drank from goblets of gold.

During the season of the Lenten fast, if he had connections with the Church, or wished it to be widely known that he was devout, he temporarily replaced his golden dishes and goblets with silver ones— the humblest form of table-ware to which he was prepared to demean himself! The records of gold plate which the wealthy of the Middle Ages and later possessed make astonishing reading. Louis d'Anjou, for instance, kept in constant use more than 260 pieces of enamelled gold table-ware, and 2,000 pieces of enamelled silver-gilt.

Throughout Europe, the cult of ostentation is to be found, varying in degree and style from country to country, but dependent primarily on the art of the goldsmith, who had learned his trade indirectly from the Romans, the Etruscans, the Greeks, the Egyptians, down the centuries. In Germany, France, Holland, Britain, Italy and elsewhere, men with sufficient means employed goldsmiths to produce for them objects in the precious metal which would enable them to hold their heads high when they entertained. They had, no doubt, read their Bible, and in their own day, a thousand years after the birth of Christ, wished somehow to emulate the wealth of Solomon, who had lived a thousand years before Christ; such verses as these must have filled them with envy:

Now the weight of gold that came to Solomon in one year was six hundred, three score and six talents of gold. [They may have known that the talent represented about £240 sterling.] King Solomon made two hundred targets of beaten gold, six hundred shekels of gold went to one target. And he made three hundred shields of beaten gold; three pounds of gold went to one shield. Moreover the king made a great throne of ivory and overlaid it with the best gold. And all King Solomon's drinking-vessels were of gold, and all the vessels of the house were of pure gold; none were of silver, for it was nothing accounted of in the days of Solomon. . . .

They could not, of course, hope to compete with this magnificence. Nevertheless, they could afford a good deal, and their patronage of the goldsmiths was one of the nobler forms of patronage. Goldsmiths flourished; the names of some of them have become household words wherever the goldsmith's art is spoken of. Hugo d'Oignies is one of them; another is Van Vianen. Lutmas, Schongauer and the Roettiers are others; and Giovanni di Bartolo,

Benvenuto Cellini and Ugolini di Vieri. These are among the great names of men who took that most malleable and rewarding of precious metals, the one most coveted by man for thousands upon thousands of years, and brought to its manipulation their skill and imagination and inherent appreciation of the potentialities of rare metal, and wrought the *objets d'art* which today fill the display cabinets of the world's museums and delight the eye and exalt the spirit.

Closely allied to the art of the goldsmith is, of course, the art of using gold-leaf—the product of the gold-beater. This, too, is a very ancient art: it was certainly practised by the Egyptians five thousand years and more ago. They used gold-leaf both for the adornment of statues and for the more intimate adornment of tombs and mummy-cases. One of the most beautiful of these last is that of the Theban king, An-Antef, who died in 2600 B.C.; it may be seen in all its perfection after four and a half millennia in the British Museum today.

From Homer, writing three thousand years ago, we learn that gold-leaf was frequently used for the gilding of the horns of sacrificial cattle; and though the art of using gold-leaf, and the art of gold-beating, are both of Egyptian origin, it is not surprising that the twin arts spread westwards by way of Greece to Rome and Italy and Europe generally. In the first century A.D. Pliny described how gold-leaf was used for the ornamentation of some of the pillars and other architectural features of great edifices like the Capitol in Rome. Patrician wives demanded gilding on the framework of their beds as evidence of their exclusive status; and there is an entertaining parallel to this whim to be found among the patrician wives of New York nearly two thousand years later.

With his interest in detail generally, Pliny gives a revealing account of the gold-beater's art. In his day, a single ounce of gold could be beaten into no fewer than 750 leaves, each of them "four fingers" square; but even gold-leaf as fine as that was something like three times as substantial as the gold-leaf of later gold-beaters! Certainly an interesting aspect of gold-leaf is the fact that the method of its preparation has remained virtually unchanged, even in detail, since the very earliest times: there can surely be few crafts that have been practised in the same manner over a span of as much as five thousand years. Pictures, inscriptions and carvings, as well as occasional written records such as those of Pliny, prove this; and much of the gilding on Egyptian mummy-cases reveals that the skill of the gold-beater in those far-off days was as great as that of the Italian and other European gold-beaters at their finest. To watch a contemporary gold-beater at work is to be a spectator at a fascinating process which has retained its individuality over a formidable expanse of time.

Today, pure gold is considered too soft for the many commercial purposes to which it is applied. A gold alloy, therefore, is ordinarily prepared, in which both copper and silver are introduced in such a way as to produce 23- or 24-carat gold. As from the beginning, the first stage in the actual preparing of the gold-leaf is to melt this gold in a crucible and run it off into a mould which will produce an ingot, usually about five inches long, an inch or slightly more wide and varying in thickness between an eighth and nearly half an inch. The ingot is then passed through a succession of steel rollers under varying degrees of pressure, until it has been transformed into a continuous ribbon anything up to 120 feet long and approximately one-thousandth of an inch thick. Only now it is thin enough to be passed on to the actual gold-beater for his skilled attention.

He receives it in the form of many hundreds of one-inch squares, already so thin that from this point onwards they must not be touched by hand but only by a pair of boxwood tongs. With these tongs he carefully inserts two hundred of these inch squares between leaves of very fine vellum, four inches square. These alternating leaves of gold and vellum constitute a square package which he refers to as his "cutch". He binds the whole together with thin strips of parchment and lays it on his "anvil", preparatory to beginning the long-drawn-out beating process.

His anvil is one of the traditional pieces of equipment which have remained almost unchanged down the fifty centuries during which the gold-beater has practised his art. It consists of a cube of granite or marble, mounted at a height convenient to himself on a stout pillar of wood driven deep into the workshop floor. The reason for the massiveness of the stone and the sturdiness of the timber pedestal is to reduce so far as possible the vibration resulting from the many hours of beating with heavy hammers which the anvil is designed to endure.

Having laid the cutch squarely in the centre of the anvil, the gold-beater takes up the first of a succession of specially designed hammers. It weighs some 17 lbs. and consists of a short wooden handle driven into a cast-iron head with two faces, each one four inches across and very slightly convex. This is the hammer still to be seen, though very rarely, alas, mounted above the entrance to a gold-beater's premises: a heavy hammer gripped by a powerful hand belonging to a thick-set, muscular forearm.

To wield, one-handed, a 17-lb. hammer for any length of time would be more than even the most muscular arm could manage; but thanks to the solidity of the anvil and the resilience of the vellum skins composing the cutch, the hammer is, in fact, given a quite considerable upward reaction from each downward blow. The gold-beater's hammer—which is in fact an extension of his arm—rapidly achieves a rhythmic rise-and-fall at an undeviating rate of approximately fifty blows per minute. And while the hammer rises and falls, the cutch is systematically turned on the anvil so that the regular blows fall uniformly on every part of it. The operation may look simple but a gold-beater will tell you that he had served an apprenticeship of as much as seven years before he had mastered even this initial stage of his trade.

At the end of half an hour's steady beating, the inch square of gold-leaf will have spread uniformly outwards, and now a fine edge will be glinting along each of the four sides of the cutch between each vellum skin and the one above and below it. The gold-beater now lays aside his 17-lb. hammer, carefully unties the parchment binding and opens the cutch. He takes out each leaf in turn and, with his boxwood tongs, lays it on a calfskin cushion. Then, with an extremely sharp-bladed "skewing-knife" he cuts each individual leaf into four squares, reducing them almost to their original area. Though they have their original area, however, they are now many times thinner than they were when the hammering began: so thin, in fact, that when he makes up his "book" of skins for the second time, eight hundred squares of gold-leaf between eight hundred leaves, or "gold-beaters' skins", constitute a package less than an inch in thickness!

For this second "book", which he refers to as a "shoder", he uses not vellum but an extremely fine, tough skin which is, in fact, a membrane forming the outer coat of the *caecum*, or great intestine, of an ox. This membrane is extremely costly. Only a few gold-beaters' skins can be obtained from one animal, and since every shoder requires eight hundred of these, it may be seen what a demand this makes on supply. To obtain sufficient for one shoder, some three to four hundred ox-guts are required. Each membrane is freed from adhering fat, stretched on a frame and treated first with a solution of aromatic substances in isinglass and then with white of egg. When it is fully prepared it is so strong, in spite of its extraordinary thinness, that it will endure approximately a thousand hours of beating before it can be relied upon no longer for this important stage in the processing of gold-leaf. A gold-beater reckons each of these skins to be worth exactly as much as the square of gold-leaf he lays upon it!

The shoder, approximately 4½ inches square, is now laid upon the anvil and beaten with a shodering-hammer weighing a mere 12 lbs. But it is beaten for between two and three hours, by the end of which time once again the pale glint of gold-leaf is seen along its four edges. The second, but still not the last, stage in the process has come to an end.

The gold-beater unpacks his shoder, moving with infinite care, for now the leaves are so gossamer thin that the slightest breath would send them flying. They are too thin, now, to be cut by the finely-tempered steel blade of his skewing-knife. Instead, they must be cut with a curious instrument known as a "wagon". It consists of a miniature sledge fitted with a pair of extremely sharp "runners" made, curiously enough, of the finest Malacca cane. Since bamboo and most varieties of cane are essentially oriental products it is to be assumed that the earliest gold-beaters used cane for cutting the leaves; apparently no better blade for this delicate work has been devised by inventive man in all the centuries that have followed.

With his calfskin cushion and cane knife, the gold-beater once again quarters his gold-leaf, running the "wagon" to and fro across it until he has obtained four two-inch squares from each. They are now, of course, thinner than ever; but they are not yet thin enough for the gold-beater. There is to be a final beating, after preparatory treatment.

Each leaf is individually dusted with an extremely fine powder known as "brime". And here again the method of dusting it is an unexpected one. In spite of many experiments, nothing more suitable for dusting the gold-leaf has been found than the old method: the hind foot of a hare! When the 800 gold-leaves have been dusted, they are then interleaved between the same number of skins and made up into a third "book", known to the gold-beater as his "mould". It is laid on the anvil and then beaten for anything up to six hours with the lightest of the gold-beater's hammers: one weighing a mere 8 lbs.

When for the third time the glint of pale gold is seen along the four sides of the mould, the craftsman lays aside his hammer and with infinite care proceeds to open it. So thin are the gold-leaves, now, that the only way in which they can be spread flat on the calfskin cushion for trimming with the wagon is by a deft and expertly calculated puff of air from between pursed lips. Even this minor operation calls for the maximum degree of expertise: a fraction too hard, a fraction too much on the slant, and the gold-leaf is ruined.

It is now almost unbelievably thin: something in the order of three-millionths of an inch. Twelve hours previously, it was a strip emerging from between smooth steel rollers, approximately one-thousandth of an inch in thickness. The final reduction to this infinitesimally small fraction has been effected entirely by the skilled application of a succession of graduated heavy hammers wielded by a craftsman who has spent many years mastering his craft.

It is interesting to compare the different figures which have been given over the centuries in connection with this ultra-refinement of gold-leaf. Pliny, writing some nineteen centuries ago, stated that one ounce of gold could be beaten into 750 leaves, each of them about three inches square. This represents approximately 54 square feet of gold-leaf from one ounce. According to a seventeenth-century note, contemporary gold-beaters three hundred years ago could produce gold-leaf from one ounce of gold which, if it were possible to maintain it in a single, unbroken sheet, would cover an area of 105 square feet—almost twice as much as Pliny's contemporaries. A century later, that figure had been increased to $146\frac{1}{2}$ square feet. There are subsequent references to areas of 189 square feet and one of even 200 square feet. Yet it is only necessary to examine microscopically the gilding on such mummy-cases as that of King An-Antef to find that between four and five thousand years ago Egyptian gold-beaters could produce gold-leaf comparable in fineness of texture with that produced today!

The worker in gold-leaf does not, of course, set about his task with a complete "mould" in his equipment. In fact, the leaves taken by the gold-beater from his mould are trimmed and then made up into small "books" containing some twenty-five gold-leaves apiece. These suffice for all the smaller ornamentation the craftsman is called upon to do.

But there are certain demands made upon his services from time to time which parallel in the present time the large-scale use of gold-leaf of Roman and Egyptian times. It is not only the Palace of Cleopatra that was lavishly adorned with gold-leaf: it may be seen today on Buckingham Palace and Windsor Castle. On a great number of contemporary structural and architectural landmarks, too, up and down the country: St. Paul's Cathedral, for instance; Tower Bridge, the Albert Memorial, the Monument, the National Gallery, and many other public buildings. There was a Guild of Gold-Beteres in London as long ago as the twelfth century; they have been with us ever since, for there is always a demand for their expert craftsmanship.

Glasgow, too, ranks high in the craft of gold-beating. You may still see the traditional gold-beater's arm-and-hammer over a doorway in a Glasgow street, the trade-sign of a gold-beating firm that has been in the hands of one family for over a hundred years. Gold-leaf from this small firm can be found not only in the Gold Banqueting Hall in Glasgow's famous City Chambers and on the ceiling of the Hall of Sculpture in her Art Galleries, which used between them 6,000 books of gold-leaf—nearly a quarter of a million leaves in all! It has gone much further afield. This firm proudly claims that gold-leaf produced on their stone anvils by the rhythmic application of hammers wielded by Glasgow men has been used to gild the Palace of Versailles: a task so great that it occupied twenty skilled men working day and night for a whole year. And thousands of miles away to the east—in the land where gold-beating has been a tradition as long as that in almost any other part of the world—there is Glasgow gold-leaf on the incomparable Taj Mahal.

The application of gold-leaf for ornamentation, whether for such small areas as the lettering in gold of book titles, the gilding of page edges or picture-frames, or for the gilding of architectural features such as the cross above St. Paul's Cathedral or the Scales of Justice that dominate the roof-tops of the City of London, naturally demands great skill in the craftsman. Where the work is to be done on some object of great value, the gilding, in fact, being an integral part of the finished product, then the greatest possible attention must be given to detail. Much has been written about the art of preparing and laying-on gold-leaf, and perhaps no one has written better about this than some of the Italian artist-craftsmen of the *quattrocento*. Many of these were artist-craftsmen in the application of gold-leaf for gilding and ornamentation, whether of manuscripts or of paintings or of architecture generally.

One of these, Cennino Cennini, whose teacher had been a disciple of the great Giotto, set down elaborate instructions based on his own experience of the materials, for the benefit of those who had yet to learn this exacting art. Having described in minutest

detail how to prepare the panels on which the gold is to be laid
(in medieval Italian pictures it was customary to cover the panel
completely with gold-leaf before beginning to paint on it), he
proceeds to explain what to do next:

When the weather becomes damp and cloudy, place your
panel flat on two trestles. Sweep it with a feather, then burnish
it with a piece of coarse linen. If you afterwards burnish it with a
tooth—the teeth of dogs, cats, lions, wolves, leopards and
generally of all carnivorous animals are equally good—it cannot
look otherwise than well. When you have thus burnished it, put
into a glass nearly full of clean water a little of the white of egg
tempera. Mix this thoroughly with the water. Take a large
pencil of minever [fine fur], made of the hairs of the tip of the
tail. Take up your gold-leaf with a pair of fine pincers, lay it on
a square piece of card, larger than the gold-leaf, which you
hold in your left hand. With the pencil of minever in your right
hand, wet the surface sufficiently to hold the gold-leaf. Then let
the gold-leaf slip off the card. As soon as the gold-leaf touches the
wet surface, withdraw the card quickly and suddenly. If you
perceive that the gold does not adhere to the panel, press it down
gently with clean cotton.

When you have laid on three pieces, pass the cotton over the
first piece and see whether any part requires mending. Provide
a cushion as large as a brick, made of wood covered with soft
leather, very clean and not at all greasy, of the same kind as
that of which boots are made. Spread a piece of gold-leaf on the
cushion and with a knife cut it into pieces as you want them,
to make the necessary repairs. Wet the parts to be repaired
with the minever pencil and then, wetting the handle of the
pencil with your lips, the piece of gold-leaf will adhere to it
sufficiently to enable you to apply it to the part to be repaired.

When you have laid as much gold as you can burnish in one
day, be careful to collect the small pieces of gold, as those masters
do who are economical, that you may save as much gold as you
can, being sparing of it and always covering the gold you have
laid on with a clean handkerchief. And when you come to
burnish the gold on your panel you must procure a stone called
lapis amatisto. If you have not this stone, then sapphires, emeralds,
rubies, topazes and garnets are still better: the finer the stone,
the better it is for the purpose. . . .

There is a fascination in following the instructions of artist-craftsmen comparable with the fascination experienced in looking at the work which came from their nimble pens and brushes and tools-of-their-trades.

THIRTEEN

Croesus Today

"A broad and ample road, whose dust is Gold."
Milton.

"It was a sumpshous spot, all done up in gold, with
plenty of looking-glasses."
Daisy Ashford.

IN 1959 the richest man in the world was believed to be His
Highness Sir Abdullah al-Salim al-Subah, Ruler of Kuwait, whose
annual income was estimated at £111,000,000. This represents
approximately £2,150,000 every week, or very nearly £20 per
minute. It is, by any standard, a lot of money. Deriving, of
course, from "black gold", piped out of his country by way of his
pocket.

The story of how millionaires "made their piles": of their
beginnings, the successive stages in the building of their fortunes,
the manner in which they used their wealth and equally (if not
perhaps more so) abused their wealth, has always held a fascination
for others who perhaps count their fortunes in pence and silver
rather than in gold. Biographies of Croesus in whatever age he
adorned have never been lacking; autobiographies are less
numerous: possibly because the wealthiest men rarely have time
to devote to reporting; their whole and undivided attention must
be devoted to the more important act of acquisition.

In the last decade or so of the nineteenth century an anonymous
contributor to *Titbits*, evidently fascinated by the whole question
of men's wealth, and with a flair for analysis and vivid presentation
of statistics, wrote a series of articles in which he considered
"Twenty-seven of the Wealthiest Men in the World". His title, if
slightly more wordy than is the vogue today, was certainly to the
point: *Millionaires, and How They Became So.* His articles were
subsequently collected between a pair of stiff covers and published
at the modest price—particularly modest in view of the contents!—
of sixpence.

We do not propose to preach the "gospel of greed" [he says right at the outset], but rather to tell the method of success. Every true man has a laudable desire to become rich. In our efforts to assist our readers to accomplish this end, we shall give the actual methods by which colossal fortunes have been accumulated. No doubt much of it has been got by doubtful schemes, but that *will not deprive it of its interest*—and *may* serve as a warning to others!

This enterprising researcher and analyst then proceeds to draw up a list of almost a score of British millionaires, followed by a number of millionaires from the other side of the Atlantic. Research today might lead to somewhat different results, for the number of millionaires in America today is very much greater than the number in Britain. In 1959 it was calculated that America had no fewer than 8,000 dollar-millionaires; the number of millionaires in this country can probably be counted on the fingers of a maimed hand. But in the second half of the nineteenth century there were believed to be two hundred British millionaires, to less than a hundred in America.

Among his native millionaires he included David Baxter, the Dundee ironmaster, bankers such as Wolverton and Baring, the Dukes of Portland, Westminster, Northumberland and Sutherland, the Marquis of Bute, the Earl of Dysart and Baron Rothschild. Conspicuous among the lesser flock of American millionaires he included the almost legendary railway king, Jay Gould, who retired before he was fifty years old with a nice little fortune of 100,000,000 dollars, all amassed in less than twenty-five years. Others in his select list were Jacob Astor, Mackey, Girard, Cooper and Vanderbilt, all of whom possessed seven- or eight-figure fortunes.

But he realized that fortunes which run into figures normally only comprehensible to astronomers mean relatively little to the ordinary reader—the reader, that is, for whom *Titbits* catered. He therefore went to the trouble of breaking down these figures, so that they might possess some meaning for his readers.

Jay Gould's fortune, for instance, stood at one time at £55,000,000. This figure, virtually meaningless as it stands, begins to make sense when it is seen that it represents an income of £7,700 per day, £320 per hour, or £5 6s. 8d. per minute! By comparison, Rothschild's income was only £4 per minute; that of the Duke of Westminster only 30 shillings; and the Marquis of Bute received a miserly 7 shillings for every "sixty seconds' worth of distance run".

(Certainly they were poor men by comparison with the Ruler of Kuwait!)

"These calculations," the *Titbits* man went on to emphasize, "may not be fractionally correct; we simply wish to present a table giving an idea of the enormous fortunes, so that anyone can at a glance learn the interesting details thereof." Interesting they certainly are; and either stimulating or depressing according to the latent ambition and opportunity (or lack of it) of the fascinated reader.

Certainly, too, the stories of how these millionaires and multi-millionaires rose from comparative penury—the traditional dime-in-the-pocket-and-turned-out-of-the-home theme being well to the fore—to these fantastic pinnacles of monetary success make engrossing reading. Andrew Carnegie, for instance, at the age of eleven was earning tenpence a day as a bobbin-boy in a cotton mill. By the time he had reached the age of sixty-one he had sold his business interests for 500,000,000 dollars; when he died, in 1919, it was estimated that during his lifetime he had donated no less than 300,000,000 dollars to various philanthropic institutions.

Three other multi-millionaires illustrate the same fabulous theme. Armour, the Chicago meat-packer, started life as an ill-paid farm-hand; within thirty years he owned a business with an annual turnover of more than £20,000,000. James Doyle started as a small-town drugstore clerk; he was still only middle-aged when he could turn down an offer for £10,000,000 for one of his properties. John A. Wanamaker, the store king, was an errand-boy earning two shillings a day while Daniel Fayerweather, the leather king, was a tin pedlar; both became multi-millionaires, for everything they touched turned to gold.

The Scot, James Baird, like Armour, started work as a farm-hand; by the time he reached middle-age his annual income was almost a million pounds. Jay Gould, who retired from business before he was fifty, was turned out of his home at the tender age of twelve with two shillings in the pocket of a new pair of knickerbockers and told to make his own way in life. The list can be almost indefinitely extended; and on both sides of the Atlantic. And the men under consideration were handling *gold*, as well as stocks and shares and properties.

Outstanding among the wealthiest American families for three or four generations, of course, have been the Rockefellers. It was said that John Davison Rockefeller, Sen., who had begun life as a junior clerk, was the richest man in the world except for the

Aga Khan when he died at the ripe old age of ninety-eight. His fortune was in the region of 1,000,000,000 dollars—a figure representing wealth very much greater at that date, just before the war, when he died, than it would be today; but in any case one so astronomical that it staggers the mind even to contemplate it.

J. D. Rockefeller, of course, was one of the greatest philanthropists the world has ever known. When he was still in his mid-sixties, before he had embarked on the noble series of philanthropic gestures for which he and his son will always be remembered, his fortune stood at some £50,000,000. In the single year 1900 it increased by a further £15,000,000. This figure so astonished a contemporary journalist (who perhaps should have known better than to register surprise at anything involving the Rockefellers and their money) that it set him doing some calculations. He duly reported as follows:

> This is the equivalent of 118 *tons* of gold, at the price of gold prevailing in the United States of America. It is as much gold as a thousand strong men could lift, if each one of them were to lift considerably more than two hundredweight at a time. It represents as many sovereigns as would be required to carpet *two acres* of ground!

But Rockefeller, unlike many multi-millionaires, was no miser. He established the famous Rockefeller Foundation and endowed it so munificently that in the first thirty years of its existence alone a total of 360,000,000 dollars passed from it by various channels to deserving causes. Nevertheless, thanks to Rockefeller its assets at the end of that period still stood at no less than 138,000,000 dollars! The story of the Rockefeller Foundation is one of the great stories of great wealth nobly distributed.

Rockefeller's may be the greatest name in this respect, but it is by no means the only one. Another is that of Cornelius Vanderbilt. He started life as a farm-hand—the traditional "hired man". His first venture into private enterprise was when he established a very modest ferry service at a point at which such a service had long been badly needed. Indeed, ferry services seem to have been something of an obsession with him in the early years of his life; for by the time he reached middle-age he had developed them on such a scale that he could, when at last he felt like selling out, pick his buyer: one of these enterprises of his changed hands for the sum of 10,000,000 dollars!

Like Rockefeller, he gave away enormous sums of money. An example of this, only one among a considerable number, is the 1,000,000 dollars which he gave to a New York educational institution which, in gratitude, thereupon changed its name to Vanderbilt University. Yet in spite of vast donations such as this, when old Cornelius Vanderbilt died at the age of eighty-three he was still worth more than 100,000,000 dollars. This entire fortune he bequeathed to his son, William Henry. And William Henry, who inherited his father's generosity as well as his wealth, and throughout a long life made a succession of notable philanthropic gestures, had sufficient business acumen to double those 100,000,000 dollars in spite of the constant drain on them.

When money flows in such spate it presents problems. Even if you are philanthropically-minded, like Rockefeller and Vanderbilt and some others of their peers; even if you plough back millions upon millions into the multifarious enterprises which yield the ever-increasing wealth; even if you launch out in all directions and acquire other flourishing enterprises and bring them in "beneath the umbrella": yet millions remain to be dealt with. In the case of millionaires, and still more with multi-millionaires, money tends to breed money; the tide is a one-way tide, with no ebb to counteract its swelling volume.

It is not unnatural, therefore, that these men have for long sought to establish themselves in such a way that they—or at any rate their womenfolk—may have some standing in the society of their day. And how better than by building magnificent dwellings for them and filling these with artistic treasures that only the deepest purses can buy? The story of Fifth Avenue offers an epitome of this very natural and by no means reprehensible attitude of mind.

By the turn of last century, Fifth Avenue, New York, was the address of some fifty palatial edifices designed and erected for American multi-millionaires. In those days building materials and labour costs were still, even in the United States, relatively small by today's standards; yet it has been calculated that the homes of the Croesus's of Fifth Avenue represented a total outlay of well over £20,000,000, while the total fortunes of their chief occupants represented a good deal more than £500,000,000. And these are pounds sterling, not mere dollars.

Outstanding among them was the home built for Cornelius Vanderbilt. It was modelled on the famous Château de Blois and stood at the junction of Fifth Avenue and 57th Street—an odd thought, incidentally, to have a château at a road junction! The fabric alone cost Vanderbilt well over £1,000,000, and in addition to this a house which he considered uncomfortably close to it was bought for £25,000, completely gutted, and then rebuilt in such a way as to be capable of incorporation into the new structure—at a further cost of over £70,000.

A little further along what came to be popularly referred to as "Millionaires' Mile" a former clerk in a flour mill and now the street-railroad king spent £1,000,000 on the erection of a Fifth Avenue palace. The details of Charles T. Yerkes's expenditure make almost unbelievable reading. On the bathroom attached to the best bedroom he spent £60,000; the bedstead designed for his wife cost £2,000—and has not been paralleled since until, perhaps, the occasion of the recent Furniture Exhibition, with its fantastic all-purpose-self-operating-musically-televisionally-equipped-and-what-have-you bed gave some ingenious-minded furniture maker an opportunity to show what the present century can offer. Just in case visitors might be inclined to feel that an outlay so extravagant was a little vulgar, Yerkes ordered pictures, statues and *objets d'art* to a total of £500,000 to be delivered to his palace when it was completed, and had these displayed in lavishly appointed cabinets!

Another multi-millionaire who, so to speak, rubbed shoulders on Fifth Avenue with the Vanderbilts, Astors, Yerkes and their neighbours frequenting "Millionaires' Mile" was Senator Clark, a self-styled "Copper King". He erected for himself and family a five-storey palace of white marble. Into it he packed a million dollars-worth of Oriental divans, carpets, cabinets and assorted bric-à-brac; on the marble tiled floor of what he referred to as the Oriental Room he spread a single Persian carpet for which his agent in the East had paid £8,000. The New York sunlight shone on to this twentieth-century Aladdin's Cave through windows of Damascus glass for which another of his indefatigable agents had paid £3,000.

It was, in fact, the furnishings and fittings of these Fifth Avenue palaces which, when they were made public, caught the fancy and tickled the taste of those who lived more modestly. Figures in millions they had difficulty in digesting; that such-and-such a dwelling had cost one, two, three millions meant nothing. But that Mrs. Charles T. Yerkes was sleeping in a £2,000 bed and making her toilet in a £60,000 bathroom; that Senator Clark had an £8,000 carpet on the floor of one room and £3,000-worth of glass in his window-frames; that Jacob Astor's butler had the care of a solid gold dinner service valued at over £12,000: details such as these could be taken in, comprehended and mulled over or inveighed against at one's leisure!

One of the accounts of individual luxury which particularly caught the popular fancy was that describing how Stephen S. Marchand had furnished his palace on Fifth Avenue. Marchand was a man who liked to plan on the heroic scale. He had heard the story of his neighbour, Charles T. Yerkes, who had spent a cool £2,000 on a bedstead for Mrs. Yerkes; very well, then: he would go one better than this—and the world should be told about it!

He engaged a number of artist-craftsmen to design and construct a bed for Mrs. Marchand—a bed to out-do all beds in the past, whether those constructed for Solomon and his concubines, for the Queen of Sheba, for Tutankhamen or for any other sybaritic sleeper down the ages. It was made in the main of ivory and ebony. In order to have ivory of the right age, type, weight and hue for the ornamentation of the head of the bedstead alone, a team of elephant hunters was dispatched on safari into the African jungle to collect. When they returned, he wrote out a cheque for £4,000 in settlement of their expenses and fees, and the ivory was handed over to his craftsmen for working.

The hangings of the bedstead were of a specially designed purple damask, woven specially for him on French looms; the cost per yard would have kept an average American family in rent, food and clothing for several weeks. The bedstead, when finally completed, had cost Marchand, one way and another, some £38,000—nearly twenty times what Yerkes had paid for his own wife's bed. This realization afforded him the utmost gratification.

The bedroom, of course, had to be proportionate and in keeping with the bed it was to house. It had carved and heavily gilded panels on all its walls, which alone cost some £12,000. It had purple-and-gold Genoese velvet curtains on all its great windows. The ceiling was painted by experts in the art brought over from Paris specially for the purpose, and cost Marchand a further £4,000. There were under-curtains of hand-woven Brussels net, interwoven with silk, that cost him £3,000.

As to essential bedroom furniture, other than the fabulously ornate and expensive bedstead: money was still no object. The washstand, wardrobe and dressing-table cost Marchand £50,000; the bedroom chairs, fashioned of solid carved ivory inlaid with ebony and ornamented with insets of gold, cost him £8,000; the double-doors leading into and out of the bedroom, together with their fittings, cost him £3,000. Marchand's total outlay on this bedroom and its contents was a little over £193,000. One may feel confident that he saw to it that these figures came eventually to the ears of Messrs. Astor, Clark and the rest of them; and particularly to those of Charles T. Yerkes. If they were on visiting terms, it may have been amusing when Mrs. Yerkes and Mrs. Marchand compared notes; and even more so when, afterwards, they had it out with their respective husbands!

They would not be the only people to find stirred within themselves the ignoble emotions so often stirred by the sight of gold in someone else's possession. There were many worthy American housewives, living in humbler homes, who would read about these fantastically extravagant expenditures on carpets, chairs and curtains, glance at their own furnishings, and ask themselves (and their long-suffering husbands) whether there was such a thing as justice on this earth. On earth? If they ever dared to set foot on the pavements of "Millionaires' Mile" they may have gained the impression that for the moment they were not walking on earth at all but in some celestial sphere whose inhabitants lived their remote lives in a dimension completely different from the one to which they themselves were accustomed. And they could hardly be blamed for thinking that way.

How these lordly ones in their super-luxury palaces delighted to entertain, too! How they vied with one another in the lavishness and splendour of their spending! Details of this kind, also, had the habit of becoming public property in due course: and infuriating as well as exciting the hearers.

There was, for example, the famous—or notorious—"Swan Dinner", given by a certain Mr. Luckmeyer. Seventy-five carefully selected guests sat down to it. The centre of the great table was occupied by a miniature lake on which live swans and cygnets leisurely paddled and preened their feathers. The banquet itself consisted of nine courses, each consisting of delicacies so rare that each had had to be specially obtained from a different part of the world. The most distinguished European chefs were engaged in the preparation of the banquet. Luckmeyer spent £2,500 on it, which worked out at an average of £35 for each of his seventy-five guests.

For a time, of course, the Swan Dinner was the talk of the town; but inevitably it was superseded. For sheer originality, for splendour, for exclusiveness—only twenty-three guests were invited this time—and for sheer cost-per-head (the criterion, it would appear, of distinction in these matters), George A. Kessler's famous "Gondola

Banquet" handsomely eclipsed Luckmeyer's effort, and indeed all others that had preceded it. Moreover, it had another claim to distinction: the whole splendiferous affair was planned and executed in twenty-four hours!

Kessler demanded the best of everything. He could well afford it, and from the outset made it clear to all contractors and sub-contractors that so far as cost-per-honoured-guest was concerned, the sky was the limit.

So, a team of twenty expert scene-painters was engaged and set to painting a complete Venetian scene, and it was made clear to them that unless it included an Italian campanile it would not be considered complete. Lighting engineers were commissioned to prepare special lighting effects, and these had to include an electric moon and an electric firmament. The number of individual stars and planets was not stipulated, but when the time came it seemed to the guests that everything was in position save possibly the Milky Way!

A whole courtyard was made watertight by the installation of concrete dams and walls, and then filled with water. A flotilla of Venetian gondolas was constructed from illustrations studied at an art gallery. Some of these were full-size, for the use of the guests; others, smaller scale-models correct in every detail like the full-size ones, for the use of the waiters conveying food and drink between kitchens and table. A troupe of waiters was hired. Each man was individually measured and fitted out as a gondolier, and while their costumes were receiving their finishing touches they were quickly trained in the art of handling gondolas. Many hundreds of pounds-worth of hot-house roses and carnations were ordered from the florists.

Twenty chefs, each one an expert in one specific province of the culinary art, were engaged on the preparation of the banquet, assisted by a covey of skilled assistants. The most memorable feature of the banquet, it was reported afterwards, was the Ice Course. A contemporary account, doubtless circulated deliberately through the right channels so as to reach the greatest number of people likely to be suitably impressed, reads as follows:

M. Scrapi carved three great Lions of Venice, all in ice, which were borne in upon the shoulders of gondolier-waiters and formed a conspicuous feature of the culinary pageant. The Venetian Lions themselves each bore a tray, upon which were iced peaches. The other details included the wonderful cake, over five feet in

height, which was brought in upon the back of Jumbo Jr., the
baby elephant. Not only was the cake lit up all over by electric
light, but it was set upon a revolving platform. . . .

Compared with Luckmeyer's Swan Dinner, at which some £35
was spent per head, Kessler's Gondola Banquet was indeed a
triumph. The cost per head was duly announced as £125—very
nearly four times what his rival had spent. But surely, far more
remarkable than the lavishness of the meal, than even the wonder of
M. Scrapi's ice-confection, is the fact that all this was achieved
within twenty-four hours. George A. Kessler must have been a
remarkably efficient organizer; or, as is more probable, brilliantly
successful in the art of getting other people, in their respective
spheres of competence, to get things moving on his behalf. It is
wonderful what a hint of gold can do.

FOURTEEN

Gamblers' Gold

"There are two times in a man's life when he should not speculate:
when he cannot afford it—and when he can."

Mark Twain.

"And once or twice to throw the dice
Is a gentlemanly game. . . ."

Oscar Wilde.

WITH the possible exception of the Australian gold-fields there is
probably no place on earth where gold has changed hands more
dramatically than at the tables of Monte Carlo. There, in the days
when gold was the common currency, when every businessman
carried sovereigns as today he carries his cheque-book and small
boys at prep. schools received "half-sovs." from visiting indulgent
uncles, gold was the stake and gold the prize. Gold glittered on the
tables, emphasizing the whole atmosphere of cupidity amounting
to lust, cut-throat competition and callousness to others' losses.
Gold was the lure; and the lust it excited and the disillusion and
bitterness its loss promoted were inseparable from the unpredictable
spinning of a small, ingeniously devised and delicately constructed
mechanical object, the roulette wheel. Whole books have been
written about the vagaries of fortune encountered by the men and
women who throng the roulette and *trente-et-quarante* and other tables.

It used to be said at Monte Carlo: "Black often loses; Red often
loses; *White never loses.*" There is significance in the saying: it was,
of course, originally expressed in French, and the last of the three
colours, in the original, was—*blanc*. M. Blanc happens to be the
name of the founder and prime mover of Monte Carlo's casino. His
was the "bank"; and in the long run the bank is never the
ultimate loser. Though the assertion may seem over-confident, it
is a simple statement of fact: the occasions on which the bank has
been "broken" are rare indeed; and it possesses its own methods
of recouping its losses.

There have, it is true, been a certain number of gamblers at
Monte Carlo whose run of luck has been so unusual and so consistent,
whose hauls of gold have been so fantastically high, that M. Blanc

and his assistants have momentarily feared for their bank. An inveterate gambler named Senor Garcia, for instance, once swiped £40,000 from the table; and this not in a succession of lucky days but in one short session that lasted less than sixty minutes!

An English milord of those palmy days when milords still had incomes greater than those of miners, dockyard workers, stevedores and window-cleaners mulcted the casino of £30,000; while an American playing at an adjoining table pocketed £28,000. It might have been a thoroughly bad day for the bank, for the Englishman was prudent enough to leave the premises with his winnings intact; the American, however, was imprudent enough to continue playing, and in rather less time than it had taken him to win that comfortable sum, lost the lot! But he took a fresh breath, borrowed sufficient for a stake of the requisite proportions, and in four consecutive sessions won back his original prize plus some £4,000 by way of bonus; and this in four neat sums of £8,000 a time. It was, after all, a bad day for the bank.

In the casino files there is to be found the record of a gambler who was so successful at the tables that he came to be popularly known as Monte Carlo Wells. In two comparatively short bouts of play, in which he staked the maximum permitted each time, he netted a cool £50,000. There is, however, a certain complacency evident in the footnote to this particular entry. Not content with his spectacular winnings, Monte Carlo Wells played on; and, as is the way in such cases of tempting Providence, in a comparatively short time lost every penny of his £50,000 and a good deal more besides.

Another "regular" whom the casino authorities remember with mixed feelings was an American, one Colonel Power. His first hours, even his first few days, in the gaming-rooms were not remarkable; except perhaps for the fact that by contrast with the majority of gamblers he seemed extraordinarily casual. Unlike them, he bore no fanatical gleam in his eye; indeed, he appeared to have no real purpose in being there. He merely wandered about, cocking an eye at one table, ignoring another, seeming to brood within himself, and then waking up to the circumstances in which he found himself and venturing ten gold pieces here, twenty there, another ten somewhere else. His stakes were always somewhere near the minimum permitted.

Nevertheless, it soon became apparent to the croupiers, as to the other players, that the colonel *always* won. In spite of his disarming casualness, his seeming lack of any genuine interest, his money was always staked on the numbers that turned up. At the end of his first few hours of this dilettante play he had netted some 84,000 francs—and the franc, then, was worth something! However, by Monte Carlo standards it was not much: his winnings represented no more than £3,360.

He seemed to be enjoying the atmosphere prevailing at the tables, however, and the *habitués* were not surprised to see him return the following day. He stayed only an hour or two, and went away the richer by about £600. This was chicken-feed, and the croupiers hardly noticed it. Nor were they impressed by the fact that on his third day the colonel collected £1,000; and the fact that on the following day his winnings were barely half that sum convinced them that they had in fact little to worry about. One of them did, however, observe to his colleagues that, though his winnings were always small, in fact this dilettante colonel *never* lost. Hard-bitten as the croupiers were, they would have been happier if the colonel had taken himself elsewhere. M. Blanc became restless; the colonel, with his deceptive air of not really bothering much whether he won or not, continued to play, and to pick up his odd hundreds and thousands as though picking flowers in a garden.

And there came the day remembered by many as Black Friday. On that day Colonel Power unexpectedly raised his stakes to the maximum sum permitted, which was then the equivalent of £480. Surely now the gods who look down, poker-faced, on the folly of mortals who insist on being fools parted from their gold ought to have stepped in and taught the colonel a sharp lesson? But they did not. Instead, they sat, and watched from their comfortable seats above. Possibly at some time in the past M. Blanc had irked them, and they had decided it was he who must have the lesson. And certainly it was a sharp one that he received, whether the gods planned it or not. For by the end of that Black Friday Colonel Power had enriched himself at M. Blanc's expense to the tune of 1,750,000 francs. At the rate then prevailing, that was £70,000. And furthermore, the colonel had the blunt good sense to pack his bags and depart with his gold, instead of giving the bank the looked-for opportunity to regain it in its traditional manner!

Chance very obviously dominates the gaming-tables; but Chance can, and occasionally does, enter into the business in an unexpected fashion. This is well illustrated in the Monte Carlo files by the case of a Yorkshireman named Jaggers, one of the most fantastically successful roulette players ever to disconcert the croupiers and shake the substantial foundations of the bank.

He was not, like the majority of the players, a wealthy idler with nothing better to do than spend his money at the tables. He was, in fact, an artisan, a highly competent mechanic, to be precise. It is not surprising that when he first arrived he seemed hopelessly out of place among those who constituted its clientele. Indeed, it was noticeable that he did not begin to play at once; rather, he spent his time wandering from table to table, much as Colonel Power had done. But the Yorkshireman was not even laying the modest ten- and twenty-piece stakes that had been the colonel's preliminary ventures. He seemed interested solely in the roulette games; and if there had happened to be a single player at any one of the tables with an eye for anything other than his game of chance, he might have noticed that Jaggers possessed a remarkably keen eye and outstanding powers of concentration, even of penetration.

For some time he contented himself with this casual rambling among the tables. Occasionally he might have been seen to be jotting something down on a small pad he carried in his hand. But this was only after he had become a frequent onlooker at all the tables.

And then, one day, he began to play. Unlike Colonel Power's, when he did once begin his stakes were high. But like Colonel Power, he invariably backed winning numbers. In a surprisingly short time he had won no less than £120,000. This was very nearly twice as much as the colonel had won; and it might be thought that the Yorkshireman's proverbial good business sense and caution would have told him at that point to stop. Business sense he may well have possessed; caution, too. But he had, as it happened, a very good reason indeed for continuing to play; there was a *reason* for his success.

It was simply this. His expert mechanic's eye had noted the fact that each individual roulette wheel stopped more often at one particular number than at any other one—though no two wheels favoured the same number. He knew there must be a mechanical reason for this: each wheel must have some small defect or imperfection in its construction that led to its tending to do this. After a protracted tour of inspection he had duly noted the individual numbers and collated the results. His assessment of the situation paid off handsomely.

The casino authorities, however, also had mechanics in their employ, and on the night following Jaggers's tremendous wins all roulette wheels were removed from the tables and microscopically

and expertly studied. As a result, every one of them was replaced
by a new one.

The next morning, Jaggers entered the casino and started playing
the roulette tables. And for the first time since his arrival in Monte
Carlo something went wrong. Unable to believe that his first
substantial loss was anything other than a million-to-one setback,
he continued to play. Before very long he had lost one-third of his
total winnings, though all the time he had been consistently backing
the very numbers that had befriended him hitherto. When his
winnings dropped to below £80,000—which was still a good deal
more than Colonel Power had won—he accepted defeat and,
much puzzled, returned to his native Yorkshire, there to interest
himself exclusively in the pursuit of "brass", a metal which shone
less brightly than gold but was certainly much less fickle in its
behaviour towards those who handled it.

Both Jaggers and Power retained much, if not all, of the gold
they had won from the bank. Others were less fortunate; or, it may
be, less sensible. Senor Garcia, for instance, who made a haul of
£40,000 at the rate of nearly £1,000 a minute, lost it, and more,
almost as rapidly, and ended his days in destitution. Not, however,
on the casino doorstep; for the authorities very properly see to it
that the man whom they have fleeced of every penny he possessed
is given his return fare home, so that he can rot elsewhere than in
the beneficent sunshine of the Riviera.

Another gambler they remember was a Russian of the Czarist
régime. Like many of his race, he was not only an inveterate
gambler but a phenomenally successful one. His particular game
was *trente-et-quarante*. At the end of one prolonged bout of play he
had enriched himself at the bank's expense to the tune of £100,000.
Like the Yorkshireman, Jaggers, he returned the following morning
to continue his game.

It had been observed that during the first very successful day's
play he had evinced a remarkable degree of imperturbability. On
the second day, however, he seemed to be somewhat on edge. He
continued to play to some system which neither the croupiers nor
the other players had succeeded in analysing; but he was not
playing, it seemed, with quite the same degree of assurance.

Then someone offered him a cigarette, with the casual remark
that if he were to break off playing and go and smoke it in the
comparative quiet of the sunshine on the casino steps he might
possibly find that it had the effect of calming his nerves. He accepted
the cigarette, left the table, and went and smoked it, as suggested,

on the casino steps. The sun shone kindly on him—so long as he remained within its ambience. But in due course he threw the butt away and returned to the table he had left ten minutes before.

He began at once to play. The croupier noted, undoubtedly with satisfaction and possibly without surprise, that the Russian now played without any system whatsoever. His stakes were wildly made, unpredictable—and, so far as he himself was concerned, disastrous. It was not long before his £100,000 had diminished to half, to a quarter, to a negligible fraction, to nothing at all. The moment came when he did not possess the wherewithal for even the minimum stake. He had lost every penny he had won, and all the reserves with which he had commenced play!

That cigarette: had it, in fact, contained something which, far from calming the nerves, actually befuddled the brain? Was it the kindly altruistic gesture of some chance acquaintance, even of some player with, for once, a thought for someone other than himself? Or was it, perhaps, a doped cigarette strategically offered him by someone in whose interest it was to prevent further withdrawals from the bank? It is an open question.

The episode took place many years ago; in the days when gold sparkled on the gaming-tables and was a normal medium of exchange. The cynic might perhaps feel inclined to say that since the casino authorities have had every conceivable trick played upon them by the gambler dominated by the lust for gold they would be justified, once in a while, in employing their own discreet methods of checking the outward flow of gold from their coffers into the pockets of those who haunt their tables. A doped cigarette is as innocent a means as any. Certainly the Russian must have been one of those whom they were happiest to see boarding the train with a ticket in his pocket for which they themselves had paid; and Moscow was a satisfactorily long journey from Monte Carlo in any case!

There are other ways of gambling than at the tables. Fraudulent attempts to extract compensation from insurance companies by arson and other "accidents", for instance. For obvious reasons, frauds of this kind that involve gold are extremely rare today: there is not the gold in circulation between consignor and consignee which either party would be likely to use as a means to such an end. Nevertheless, there have been examples of attempts to extract compensation from insurance companies for alleged loss of gold, and in comparatively recent times. One of these is the affair in which the Turkish sailing-vessel *Mabrouk* was involved: an ingenious attempt indeed.

She came into the news—news of the kind that particularly interests brokers and underwriters—when a highly reputable firm of Paris brokers communicated with Lloyd's of London on behalf of a client of theirs. He was a merchant well known to them who had just decided to give up his highly lucrative business in Beirut and retire to his native France, where he intended to settle down and live in comfort for the remainder of his days. He had sold out very profitably and had converted the proceeds of the sale into gold bars; these he wished to ship from Beirut to Marseilles, substantially insured.

The Paris brokers asked Lloyd's, as the world's best-known and most reliable underwriters, to arrange for insurance in the sum of £75,000 to cover the shipment of gold over this relatively short voyage. Lloyd's accepted the request and proceeded to share out the cover among a number of companies with whom they normally transacted such business. The matter was quickly settled, to the satisfaction of the brokers in Paris, and certainly to that of their client. Some of those in the London offices, however, were not entirely happy about the risks involved.

This was largely because to them it seemed that there was a certain theatrical, even melodramatic, element in the information that was communicated to them from Paris. For example, it was very evident that this client was taking peculiar steps to avoid the professional interest of the Customs and other authorities in Beirut. He had told his brokers that all his gold bars would be packed into a number of barrels ostentatiously labelled "iron scrap", and that the bills of lading would echo this description. He claimed that he possessed ways of duping the authorities and thus exporting gold under their very noses. Among these means was his hiring of the unassuming Turkish sailing-vessel, *Mabrouk*, into whose holds his valuable property would be shot, rather than being loaded officially into the holds of one of the recognized Mediterranean carriers.

Rightly or wrongly, no one, it appears, made any protest at the morality or legality of what the Frenchman proposed doing, or against the unorthodox methods he was so obviously adopting to ensure the safe transit of the gold from Beirut to Marseilles; as requested, they issued the appropriate cover.

So far, so good. But it was not, they were inclined to think, so good when, almost before the shipment could have got under way from Beirut, they received a cable to the effect that the *Mabrouk* had struck a reef only a few miles off the Syrian coast and had foundered in a matter of minutes!

The suddenness of the loss, together with the fact that inquiries revealed that no reef was known to be in that area which any vessel of so light a draught as *Mabrouk's* would be likely to strike, aroused suspicions. Or it might be fairer to say, strengthened the suspicions already entertained by the underwriters. They turned, as is usual in such cases, to a professional Claims Adjuster and asked him to go out to Beirut to investigate: £75,000-worth of insurance was more than they were willing to surrender without a struggle.

There then began an extraordinary series of episodes involving the Claims Adjuster. There were false clues galore. Individuals mistakenly believed to be himself were set upon on dark nights in murky corners and were found with knives buried in them up to the hilt. There were excursions on mule back into the hinterland. There were open threats of violence, police escorts, shadowings of shadowers. There was overt and secret bribery. There was corruption and double-dealing. There was official reticence, always frustrating, and dubious advice from officialdom and other sources, public and anonymous, which contained more than a germ of danger. It was, in brief, the plot of an E. Phillips Oppenheim school novel.

The Claims Adjuster was obviously a man of mettle, courageous, persistent and wholly lacking in credulity or gullibility—to the distress of most of those with whom he came in contact during his period of investigation. He succeeded, in spite of all obstacles and very real danger to his person, in establishing a number of facts. He ran to earth, in an out-of-the-way corner, a carter who admitted, under pressure, that he had conveyed eight barrels to the Beirut quayside. They were stamped "Iron Scrap". He was able to check this in the books at the Customs office. He traced two labourers who, under the right kind of pressure, remembered that they had been employed to pack a very considerable quantity of iron bars into some barrels—they thought it might well be eight such barrels. They even contrived to remember the source of the iron bars, and the Claims Adjuster paid a visit to a Beirut blacksmith who agreed that he had recently received an order for a considerable number of iron bars, of a stipulated length, which were duly collected from him and paid for on the spot.

The master of the *Mabrouk* was traced. He appeared willing to take the Claims Adjuster out in a hired boat to the point at which, to his surprise and infinite distress, his beloved *Mabrouk* had struck this accursed reef and promptly sunk. How fortunate it was, he said, that his crew had been able to launch their one small boat and row back to Beirut without loss of life! But he became somewhat vague when they reached the spot at which, he said, his little sailing-vessel had sunk. It was here, he thought; or possibly rather further to starboard—or it might be to port—that she had sunk; perhaps a quarter of a mile away: it was difficult to remember exactly, for he had had to abandon ship so hurriedly. All he knew was that his ship had gone down beneath his very feet. Luckily, he added, he was very well insured against such loss.

The Claims Adjuster pricked up his ears at that: it was unusual, surely, for the owner of a small coastwise trader to be heavily insured. He made discreet inquiries, and learned—not entirely to his surprise—that the insurance was for a very considerable sum and that the insurer was none other than the French merchant whose gold bars were to be transported from Beirut to Marseilles so that he could live in comfort for the remainder of his days.

There were some further steps to be taken, before the report on the matter could be completed. Divers were engaged and brought to the area in which the *Mabrouk* was alleged to have sunk. They worked for a considerable time, in water of no great depth, and eventually reported themselves unable to find any trace of any sunken ship. If she had in fact sunk, then it must be somewhere else altogether; somewhere where, if she were to be located, her cargo could not be retrieved and examined by a Claims Adjuster!

By now, the expert was pretty sure that, in fact, no gold whatsoever had been involved in this case. However, he had a further means of checking this: if gold in any substantial quantity had been withdrawn by a client, one or other of the banking houses would have knowledge of the fact. He made discreet inquiries, the result of which did not surprise him in the least: to the best of the knowledge of the bankers, no quantity of gold had recently been withdrawn from their vaults by any of their clients.

He reported back to Lloyd's by cable, and returned with a sheaf of documents summarizing and substantiating his findings. On the strength of these the underwriters communicated with the brokers in Paris, to the effect that they would welcome an opportunity to discuss with their client certain puzzling aspects of the claim he had made upon them. Their reply took some time. When it did come, it was to the effect that their client regretted that owing to pressure of business he would be unable to make the journey to

London to discuss the matter of his claim. He would be glad to
have it settled at once.

Lloyd's took counsel's advice. And on the strength of this, sent a
letter to the effect that they had reason to doubt the validity of the
claim. In the circumstances, they must firmly request immediate
surrender of the policies they had made out for him. Their letter
was so worded that the Frenchman did not need to be particularly
astute to realize that the Law was on their side, not his. The policies
were put in an envelope and posted back to London. And there, in
Lloyd's offices, they were duly burned.

It was the end of the strange *Mabrouk* affair. The Frenchman had
lost whatever he had paid for the insuring of the Turkish sailing-
vessel; Lloyd's and their associates had the Claims Adjuster's fee
and expenses to meet. But compared with paying out the £75,000
insurance claim on a shipment of entirely mythical gold bars,
this was a small matter indeed. All had gambled. The stake was
considerable. On the Frenchman's part it was a criminal gamble,
and he lost outright; on the underwriters' part it was a legitimate
gamble, and they won. A survey of the gambling world, in all its
fields of activity, does not suggest that the outcome is always as
equitable as in this case!

FIFTEEN

A Fable

"What is Fame? An empty bubble;
Gold? A transient, shining trouble."
Grainger.

"Money is not required to buy one necessity of the Soul."
Thoreau.

ONCE upon a time in the Future, the peoples of the world became exasperated at the complications that seemed inseparable from the presence of gold. The chicaneries of the manipulators in the realm of high finance, the double-dealing of men in the Wall Streets of the world's cities, the international monetary manœuvring, the problems of security against theft, of safeguarding gold in transit, of equitable distribution: all these came to sicken men and women of good sense.

So, one day after long deliberation they gathered together all the gold in the whole of the world, loaded it into the capacious hold of a well-found vessel, and had it transported to an island in the exact centre of the Pacific Ocean. There they deposited it, and deposited also an International Guard to keep an eye on it; and left with a promise that every six months an International Monetary Commission would visit the island to check the seals of the vaults. On each of these visits fresh supplies of international provisions would be brought, and the International Commission would then sail away, leaving the International Guard to their important vigil.

On one of its biannual visits, however, the pilot and navigator of the big air transport carrying the International Monetary Commission entirely failed to locate the Pacific island, experts though they were. Time and again they checked their figures, referred to their charts, studied their instruments; and every time with exactly the same result: they were flying low over the exact patch of blue water where the island should be; but the island simply was not there.

Disconcerted, but not dismayed, the International Monetary Commission instructed the pilot to turn about and make for the home airport. On arrival, the first thing they did was to go into solemn conclave. One result of their solemn deliberations was that they should inquire of the seismologists whether there had been any unusual activity in the region of the Pacific during the past six months.

There had indeed. A number of leading seismologists reported that two or three months before there had been an earthquake. Its epicentre would appear to have been in the centre of the Pacific, at approximately latitude 10° North and longitude 150° West, possibly beneath the Belknap Trench to the south of the Hawaiian Islands.

The International Monetary Commission received the information with dismay. Latitude 10° North and longitude 150° West: why, that was the identical spot where the island lay on which they had deposited the gold reserves of the entire world!

They checked with the navigator of the aircraft in which they had flown out and back: yes, it was at that point that the pilot had brought his plane down practically to sea level! It was evident to the meanest intelligence that as a result of the earthquake, the Pacific island had disintegrated, and now lay as silt at a depth of some three thousand fathoms below the surface of the ocean; and in that silt was the whole of the world's gold. It occurred to one knowledgeable member of the Commission that there was an echo of the burial-service phrase, "Dust to dust", right here: the gold, so much of which had originally been extracted from silt, had returned to silt—but at a depth at which no miner could ever be expected to retrieve it. What to do, then?

Representatives of the world's governments were summoned and met in conclave behind locked and sealed doors. Panic must at all costs be avoided. "Let us pretend," said the Chairman of the Commission, appealing to the government representatives assembled round the spacious council table, "that *nothing at all has happened*; that the *status*, in fact, is still *quo*."

And so it was unanimously agreed. The International Monetary Commission continued to send out the plane they had used from the first, its crew sworn to secrecy. And the world, strange as it must seem, went on exactly as before, complacently believing that its entire gold reserves were well and truly under lock and key. As indeed, in a sense, they were.

Index

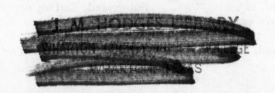